AUDIOVISUAL LIBRARIANSHIP

AUDIOVISUAL LIBRARIANSHIP

The Crusade for Media Unity (1946-1969)

LOUIS SHORES

1973

Libraries Unlimited, Inc.

Littleton, Colo.

Library of Congress Card Number 73-85472
International Standard Book Number 0-87287-076-6

LIBRARIES UNLIMITED, INC.
P.O. Box 263
Littleton, Colorado 80120

TABLE OF CONTENTS

To
LIBRARIANS, AUDIOVISUALISTS, INFORMATION SCIENTISTS,
and other colleagues in education
who have understood the theory of the Generic Book
and its applications for learning and research,

my gratitude

for their contributions during the long crusade for media unity.

INTRODUCTION: CRUSADE FOR UNITY

In 1947 there were librarians and there were audiovisualists. Many schools had libraries at one end of the hall, and audiovisual centers at the other end. Separation was fiercely advocated, not only by some library and audiovisual leaders, but by many school administrators and teachers.

That year–1947–the Florida State University Graduate School of Library Training and Service was opened. It was committed from the start to the unifying concept of "instructional materials." After two decades of crusading for this concept, and bearing a cross in both camps, for a cause that was often painfully rejected by the separatists, vindication finally came in 1969. That year, *Standards for School Media Programs* was published jointly by the American Library Association and the National Education Association. The *Standards* had been prepared by the ALA's American Association of School Librarians and the NEA's Department of Audiovisual Instruction.

The crusade for unity was not easy, because the concept was based on an abstract philosophy of communication. Contrary to the posture of some of our professional critics, there *is* philosophy in our library literature. My philosophy of the generic book is foundational for the unity concept of instructional materials, presently retitled "educational media."

The crusade for unity was not easy, because it merged, administratively, two separate units–the library and the audiovisual center–into a new organizational concept, which Florida first named "materials center." Later, other variations on the name "library" were adopted: learning resource center, media center, etc.

The crusade was most difficult of all when it came to personnel. Librarians were afraid of equipment–projectors, recorders, lenses, splicers, and a whole new world of materials. Audiovisualists without library science training had a complex about cataloging and classification, about bibliography and the minutiae of bibliographic form. When we accomplished in Florida the first unified state certification for audiovisualists and librarians, only some of us felt exaltation. The separatists continued their opposition, sensing a threat in the new breed called "instructional materials specialist," later to become the media specialist, or generalist.

Nor was the crusade easy in professional education. When Florida State opened the first graduate school of library science committed to the audiovisual education of all librarians and teachers, it embarked on a course of great promise–but also of considerable hazard.

To chronicle this crusade for unity for all of us who work in the divisions of educational media, I have gathered together in this anthology most of my shorter writings relating to the great professional conversation on audiovisualism and librarianship. My book *Instructional Materials* (Ronald, 1960) was probably the first book to undertake unification of library science and audiovisual education. In that book, also, can be found the basic media principle for the theories of Marshall McLuhan (*Understanding Media*, McGraw-Hill, 1964)–namely, *the format of the medium may affect communication.*

9

The terms generic book, media center, media specialist, and media education are the basic components of the unity concept, and are the standards on which the new AALS-DAVI program is based. What the essays in this volume reveal is something of the meaning of the crusade for unity. As the crusader who perhaps first had the vision of uniting audiovisualists and librarians in their common cause, and who has written and spoken so frequently and so much on our common mission of media learning, I want, in this introductory essay, to provide some background to both the chronicle and the concept.

ORIGIN OF THE CONCEPT

My protest against the kind of college education I was getting began in my undergraduate days, 1922 to 1926. I dissented from the meaning of liberal education as the Ivy League college defined it; I challenged, philosophically, both from the standpoint of the individual and from the standpoint of society, the higher educational theory of *elitism*, as later championed by Robert Maynard Hutchins and his disciples. But above all, I objected to the learning mode—basically, a classroom-centered education, in which group teaching, it seemed, handicapped individual learning. But instead of occupying my college's administration building, or displaying a new dimension in democratic action by walking out when the other side came up to bat, or burning a library, or identifying problems, *ad nauseam*, I decided to work on a solution—i.e., to describe my ideal college.

The idea for the kind of college I wanted to study and teach in came from Carlyle's essay on the "Hero as Man of Letters," published about 1848. Next came inspiration from a visit to Antioch College in 1928, where I observed an autonomous course in economics taught by the late, great labor arbitrator William Leiserson. These were the beginnings of my commitment to *individual, independent study* as a better learning mode than group classroom teaching. This was the beginning of the "Library-College" idea, which has now grown into an exciting movement, with its own organization, quarterly journal, convention (seven, so far), and reports from over 100 colleges that have incorporated many of the Library-College elements.

To make the individual, independent study, learning mode feasible, it seemed to me, as early as 1933, that it was necessary for the library to have a range of subjects and levels in its collection adequate to match individual differences in the students whom the college aimed to serve. This principle became basic to my college book selection, as I moved from student to teacher to librarian. Still, up to this point I had thought almost exclusively in terms of print-books, periodicals, pamphlets, documents, and the other conventional formats of my library school days.

In 1928, the Carnegie Corporation assisted a number of colleges to purchase phonograph records, later identified by audiovisualists as "discs." This made me realize that just as important as subject and level, the two cardinal criteria in book selection, was a third criterion—format. The importance of format was confirmed even in print, as I observed the different contributions of hardcover and serial publications, and fiction, reference, essay, and other literature forms. I discovered for myself the secret of encyclopedia overviewing as a learning device. Non-print, like discs and museum objects, which libraries had always stocked, suggested another dimension to independent learning, as did the visuals like slides and 16mm motion pictures, which were spearheading the new visual education movement. Convinced that these newer media could strengthen the independent study mode still further, and that libraries needed, increasingly, to stock other formats than print, I introduced at Peabody, in 1935, the first audiovisual course ever offered in the South, and certainly the first offered in a library school. An article about this offering can be found under the name of M. L. Shane, who taught the course for me. When I went off to war in 1942, the Army introduced me to some augmented concepts of audiovisual education, and I resolved that I would carry these back into my civilian professions of education and librarianship, if I came out of the war alive.

At Florida State University, where I became dean of a new library school, I had my chance. During the 1946 and 1947 planning and designing of the new school, basic audiovisual instruction was incorporated into a required course, and into units for all of the other library science courses. To reinforce instruction, a new library school library was conceived, which we named "Materials Center." Probably the first time this new name for library ever appeared in print was in a Florida State Department of Education bulletin titled *Materials Center*, edited by Sara Krentzman (Srygley), one of the first school librarians to understand the deep meaning of the unity concept, and my strongest ally for the cause on the library school faculty. Into the library school's materials center we introduced 16mm films, filmstrips, discs, tapes (wire first, when the wire recorder appeared), slides, transparencies, etc.

Our Materials Center librarian, Bessie Daughtry, who was one of our first master graduates in the new dimension library school, developed the color card catalog, with a different color for each format. Cards were intercalated with catalog cards for print. We acquired the necessary equipment for these audiovisual materials—projectors, recorders, playbacks. One of the earliest "listening posts" placed in a library reading room was introduced, with a jack and eight sets of earphones, so students could listen to John Gielgud do Hamlet's soliloquy as they read it, without disturbing readers. These were innovations for that time—1947—and the years that followed.

We got into the production of our own materials for bulletin, peg, magnetic, and flannel boards. Dioramas became a fad among our librarians and teachers in training when we started a course in "Library Graphics." Another one of our Materials Center librarians, also a master graduate of the school, Mary Alice Hunt, educated a generation of librarians and teachers in the production of posters and dioramas, slides and filmstrips, transparency overlays, discs and tapes, etc. The Library School at Florida State was taking on a different dimension.

The president of the university was so impressed by what was happening that he asked us to establish an audiovisual center for the university. This we did. It helped the university improve instruction. It also strengthened a new school on the campus. But it raised eyebrows in the library profession, and it evoked questions from the visiting team from the

ALA, looking at our new school for accreditation. Yet Florida State was one of the first three schools accredited by ALA under the new standards; and some of the members of the Board of Education for Librarianship were excited by this new audiovisual dimension in the education for librarianship.

To spread the gospel of unity among Florida librarians, audiovisualists, teachers, and administrators, a series of "leadership" conferences was inaugurated in the summer of 1947. These were followed by annual fall conferences in the Library School, jointly planned by the Florida Association of School Librarians and the Florida Audiovisual Association. An annual joint luncheon of FASL and FAVA was inaugurated at the Florida Education Association convention. Out of these meetings came the Florida unified certification, officially listed in the regulations as "Instructional Materials (Library-Audiovisual)," unique among state certifications. Through the combined efforts of librarians and audiovisualists, the Florida legislature was moved to appropriate a million dollars, earmarked for strengthening instructional materials. To orient librarians, audiovisualists, teachers, supervisors, principals, and superintendents in the unity concept, the Library School staged three annual pre-school Instructional Materials Institutes in seven strategic locations in the state. Over 1,500 people attended each of these institutes.

The institutes included a mammoth exhibit of educational media of all formats, levels, subjects; equipment demonstrations, previews, pre-auds, and browsings; and lectures by the traveling Library School faculty members and by one distinguished visiting lecturer, each of the three years. The first year it was Paul Witt; the second, it was Charles Schuller; the third, it was Amo DeBernardis, who had helped us inaugurate audiovisual instruction in the Library School, in the summer of 1947.

While we are naming outstanding audiovisualists who helped Florida State's Library School launch its innovative audiovisual education of librarians, this is a good place to record the register of audiovisualists with the unity concept. In the fall of 1947, Dr. Charles Hoban joined the Library School faculty. One of the really deep thinkers in the AV movement, Dr. Hoban had co-authored, with his father and with Zisman, the first classic textbook in the AV field. For us at Florida State, he prepared *The AV Way*, a text that one reviewer hailed as the best to that date. Through Dr. Hoban, our Library School students were introduced to the documentary film, which became an important consideration in generic book selection. Pare Lorentz' *The River*, Robert Flaherty's *Nanook of the North*, John Grierson's impressions of the herring fishermen of England, in *Drifters*, and R. H. Watt's artistic *Night Mail* began to push the hardcovers for consideration in the new dimension of library education that Florida State was pioneering.

When Dr. Hoban moved on to the University of Pennsylvania, he was succeeded by Myles Ritchie, Otis McBride, and other topnotch audiovisualists. William Quinly, who was the first to be doubly trained in library science and audiovisual education, subsequently headed the Media Center for the University. Visiting lecturers included Edgar Dale, who, because of his reading specialization, contributed to print liaison; Charles Schuller, Paul Witt, Walter Stone, Irene Cypher, and the late A. J. Foy-Cross. Although Florida State was making a home for the unity concept, and was bringing audiovisualists and librarians together in dialogue, the forces of separation were still very strong, not only outside, but within Florida.

One of my earliest writings for the unity concept, which appeared in the *Florida Journal of Education*, is included in this anthology under the title the FEA chose—"How to Tailor Learning. . . ." This position was immediately challenged, chiefly in Indiana, where the distinguished audiovisual leader Ole Larsen advocated separate libraries and audiovisual centers. In a friendly exchange we agreed to state our positions for Paul Reed, then editor of *Educational Screen*. My contribution is included here under Paul Reed's title, "Union Now." The debate continued, and there were as many audiovisualists for union, at first, as there were librarians. The split was even greater among teachers and administrators. At the invitation of the editor of the *NEA Journal*, I chaired a panel discussion on the issue of unity, with the school superintendents of San Francisco and of Grosse Pointe, Michigan. All three positions are included.

Despite the most advanced steps in the nation toward audiovisual-library unity, Florida suffered from periodic backsliding. These reversions to separatism were often led by newcomers to the state, in the teaching, audiovisual, and library fields, since Florida attracts so many people from other states. Again and again we would hear from some newcomer, with an air of triumph, "But we do it like this in Indiana (or New York, California, Illinois, etc.)"; and just as often one of the new breed of instructional materialists that we were developing into a new professional generation would remark untactfully, "We used to do it like that in Florida, before we knew better." Frequently, the counter-revolution was started by a commercial representative of one of the film producers, or equipment manufacturers, who was talked into believing unity would reduce his business.

But the cruelest separations of all came from die-hard librarians, insecure about these newer media, as they were then called, and especially about the equipment. To them I was a renegade who had gone over to the enemy, the audiovisualist; just as to the audiovisualist in the separatist camp I was an enemy librarian. Often the debates centered on what to call this new professional. The audiovisualist refused to be called a librarian; and, of course, the separatist librarian would drop dead before she would allow herself to be called an audiovisualist.

At one of these most heated discussions about what we should call this new breed of professional, I offered, not facetiously but quite seriously, that, since we all dealt with instructional materials, we should call ourselves "materialists." This was met, of course, with a roar of laughter and protest. Then, still trying to find a way to bring us together, I suggested that since the term "educational media" was beginning to replace "instructional materials," perhaps we might call ourselves "mediums." The reaction was something more like consternation that we might be identified as spiritualists transporting our media around on broomsticks. I still think we have a better claim on the occupation title "medium" than does the seance leader.

Despite these periodic setbacks, I continued to preach the gospel of unity at library and audiovisual meetings and, above all, to write for any professional journal that would accept my manuscripts. Part of my quantity writing, as attested by that Southern California study of the writing habits of librarians, went into this effort to unite librarians and audiovisualists in our common cause. Some of my more satirical critics referred to my crusade as "the shotgun marriage." Among my most painful disappointments were one caused by the *ALA Bulletin*, which has published so many of my writings, and one caused by DAVI's *Audiovisual Instruction*.

When "Portrait of a Materials Center" first appeared in the *Peabody Journal of Education*, one of the ALA editors saw it and asked for permission to reprint it in the *ALA Bulletin*, as the best description of this new concept of a library. It was planned for a special issue on the school library. But somewhere, a separatist or two objected, and with great embarrassment, the editor who had advocated it had to write and withdraw the invitation for a reprint of my manuscript.

For volume one, number one of *Audiovisual Instruction*, the late Harold Moreland, my faculty colleague in the library school and instructor in graphics, and I were asked to submit our study of instructional materials certification in the states of the union. Through statistical investigation in the 48 state departments, we had discovered trends toward 1) increasing attention to audiovisual education of teachers and librarians, and 2) unification of certification in about 12 states. Although the editor expressed delight at having this milestone study for the very first issue of the new journal, when that issue appeared it was without our article. Apologetically, the editor wrote that some members of the editorial board had asked for an opportunity to study the manuscript before publication. The study continued for month after month. Finally, after our reminders that we had foregone another opportunity for publication because we were loyal members of DAVI, the editor had to write, probably at a separatist's instigation, that the study was now outdated.

There were other setbacks. But there were triumphs, also. The ALA Association of College and Research Libraries finally invited me to do an article on AV dimensions for academic libraries, and then to edit an AV department in *C&RL*. In 1960, Ronald Press published my book, *Instructional Materials*, which first presented a preliminary classification of the generic book. This format classification is augmented and updated here. About this time the NEA Association for Supervision and Curriculum Development decided to enter the media movement by appointing a national Commission on Instructional Materials. It was my good fortune to serve on it with many distinguished leaders in the library, audiovisual, publishing and AV production field. Among those who came to the Commission's meeting was Marshall McLuhan, with whom I enjoyed two discussions about the theory of communications.

By the middle 1960s, the crusade for unity was moving definitely toward acceptance. A new generation of media specialists was arriving on the educational scene. They had been educated not only at Florida State, but at other places where the vision had arrived. In 1956, I was invited to Southern Illinois University by the Vice President and the Director of Libraries to advise on the separate course offerings in library and audiovisual instruction. As a result of my recommendations, a unified department was established that somewhat set the pattern for such programs. Other institutions which led in the unity concept of professional education were Purdue, under Carolyn

Whitenack's leadership; San Jose State, under the leadership of Leslie Janke, a graduate of Florida State; St. Cloud, Minnesota, with a program brilliantly unified by Luther Brown; and the University of Colorado, headed by Otis McBride, formerly of the FSU faculty. With each succeeding joint meeting of librarians and audiovisualists, new mutual understandings of the unity concept were being achieved.

The AASL-DAVI Media Standards were an inevitable culmination. Although these standards are a tremendous accomplishment, they have not yet completely realized either the Florida objective or a full understanding of the unity concept. But the Standards are probably as close to the ideal as compromises in practice will permit. Let me then briefly summarize here the four elements in the concept as I have understood them. Amplifications can be found in the essays that follow.

THE GENERIC BOOK

I have defined the generic book as *the sum total of man's communication possibilities*. From the dawn of civilization, man has communicated the record of his deeds and thoughts in a variety of ways. He has used all of his five senses to send and to receive communication; and, although we have not yet fully realized it in science, he has also used extrasenses to create art. The composite of all of man's sensory and extrasensory communication is the generic book. As I indicated in my editorial for *Saturday Review*, on the occasion of the first National Library Week (March 22, 1958), the generic book is the evidence of life.

The generic book comprises not only a full range of *subjects*, and a ladder of *levels* of maturity, but a multi-splendored galaxy of physical makeups, which we librarians call *formats*. To this point, library book selection has limited itself primarily to subject and level considerations, and only secondarily to format. Most libraries select print almost exclusively, with audiovisuals as an appendage. This can be seen by consulting such basic aids as the standard book lists for school, public, and academic libraries, and especially for special libraries. Generic book selection considers all three criteria equally, from the start. It recognizes that format may affect communication as much as subject and level.

Consequently, to such subject classifications as Dewey Decimal or Library of Congress, and such level classifications as K-6, 7-12, 13-14, etc., is added a format classification like the one I first proposed in *Instructional Materials*, which I have augmented in several places in this book. In the concept of the generic book there is no such thing as "non-book material." A film is as much a book as printed pages bound in hard covers. So also are tapes and discs; filmstrips, slides and transparencies; graphics of all kinds, ranging from boards (chalk, bulletin, peg, magnetic, flannel) through charts, graphs, pictures (flat and 3-D), and objects, which audiovisualists call "realia," and which may include specimens, models, mockups, etc.; radio and TV; computer, remote console, programmed learning devices; community resources; and, of course, textbooks, reference books, and serials. To paraphrase Gertrude Stein, in the concept of the generic book, a book is a book is a book. . . . Indeed, the format created by Gutenberg's press in the fifteenth century had been preceded by many other book formats: clay tablets, parchment and papyrus manuscripts, and so forth.

The generic book does not recognize the artificial boundary between print and AV. Indeed, neither do the audiovisualists and librarians, nor the publishers and producers of media. Both library and audiovisual literatures have claimed certain of the same formats: pictures, maps and globes, charts, slides, exhibits, discs, museum objects, etc. Encyclopedia publishers did not worry about crossing the AV boundary line when they introduced transparency overlays into the printed pages they bound together in hard covers. Just where "book" left off and "non-book" began has never been made quite clear. Some schools have even been known to house maps and globes in the library, but to charge them to the audiovisual budget. The sense of humor that has begun to creep into the debate was illustrated the other day in a junior college I visited, with audiovisual center and library across the hall from each other. The library had just purchased an electric eraser, and the librarian had posted a note above it for her neighbor's benefit: "Erases both book and non-book materials."

In the unity concept, the book includes the whole range of media formats, from ancient clay tablets through modern remote computer console. This is basic to the unity concept.

THE MEDIA CENTER

A media center acquires, processes, disseminates, and interpets media of all formats, subjects, and levels pertinent to the community it serves. It engages in generic book selection, and therefore does not treat non-print as an annex. Throughout, the media center considers all three of the basic criteria—subject, level, and format—in its selection of the materials most likely to accomplish the educational mission of its community. Its catalogs and indexes are intercalated without regard to format. Circulation includes booking of films as well as charging of all materials. Reference interprets the whole collection to its readers, cutting across format boundaries as courageously as it does now across subject and level boundaries, in an effort to accommodate the needs and backgrounds of the individual.

The true media center does not have an audiovisual department. It tends to organize more by subject and level than by format. A high school media center, for example, if it has two or three professional librarians, will not designate one as audiovisualist. Rather, it may have one staff member specialized in social science materials of all formats and levels; another in natural science; a third in language arts. Comparably, at the system echelon, instead of an assistant supervisor for audiovisual and another assistant supervisor for library, the division of labor may be assistant supervisor of elementary materials, and assistant supervisor of secondary materials; the recognition is thus of level, rather than of either subject or format.

A media-conscious school system will recognize three echelons of media service. The system echelon will be headed by a media supervisor or coordinator who will direct the media program toward an independent study learning mode. In this level of the media center will be central processing for all of the schools, media too expensive or too infrequently used to be housed in any one school (such as the film library, the computer core, etc.), the teachers' professional library, faculty, services, materials production, closed circuit television and radio, and so forth.

The building echelon media center is the new dimensional school library. It stocks the whole range of formats, subjects, and levels pertinent to the community and purpose it serves. Although the system echelon centrally acquires and processes for all of the building centers, the media center in the building makes its own selection of media and advises on processing features considered helpful to its individual mission. The building center also serves its classroom centers with rotating media deposits, and faculty and student bibliographic counselling.

In the new learning mode with an accent on independence, every classroom is basically a media center. This is the classroom echelon. Its media collection consists of two parts: a permanent library and a rotating library. The former will include basic reference, such as at least one good dictionary, an encyclopedia, an atlas, a globe, a wall map (celestial as well as terrestrial), a factbook, etc.; minimum equipment like bulletin, peg, flannel, magnetic, and chalk boards; screen, overhead, and opaque projectors, and perhaps slide and 8mm; tape recorder and disc playback; graphics like charts, dioramas, and pictures. On deposit will be a rotating collection from the building center, chosen usually in conference among librarians, teachers, and students, for specific units and projects.

This administrative overview of the media center omits many features, since it illustrates only a school-type library. But counterparts for academic, public, and special libraries are suggested in the essays that follow.

MEDIA PERSONNEL

In the unity concept, all of mankind comprises media personnel. Adults and children must be adequately sophisticated in understanding media, *per se*, so that our national mind, and our world mind, will be tough enough not to be subverted and brainwashed by the superficial and ugly. To accomplish this, our teachers must have a media understanding that they do not now receive, or at least do not receive adequately. The media unity concept sees the new breed of teacher as essentially a bibliographic counselor—one who matches with sensitivity, and even artistry, the individual differences in media with individual differences in learners. Such a teacher will change the impression of faculty in American higher education, as indicated in that classic Carnegie study by Harvie Branscomb entitled *Teaching with Books*. The next generation of teachers is destined to teach with the generic book as none of the teaching generations before ever have.

Leading the media regeneration of both laymen and teachers will be a new breed of librarian—a cross between the library-conscious teacher today and the education-conscious librarian. A cross is also called for between the traditional librarian, and the audiovisualist and information scientist. This new breed of librarian, or media specialist, or media generalist, will be less of a housekeeper and more of a media teacher of teachers, students, laymen, and specialists. His housekeeping will be done largely by the new middle level of paraprofessionals, by clericals, and by automated technology.

MEDIA EDUCATION

Whether a national plan will or will not at last emerge from the efforts of the American Library Association remains to be seen. As one of the commissioners, I proposed such a plan in my essay "The College of Library Arts, 1984" for the *Journal of Education for Librarianship*. It suggested some augmentations to the articulation efforts we first launched at Peabody in 1941. Unless the major peripherals, like audiovisualism and information science, are included in the plan from the start, we will not be preparing the next generation of media librarians adequately. Unless we plan for the library education (or media education) of the layman, the clerical, the paraprofessional, and the professional, in a continuum, without blind alleys, and with the right to move from one level to another without penalty, we will not have planned with perspective.

The essays that follow outline a plan for the media education of laymen, from birth to death; of teachers; of specialists; of media clericals and paraprofessionals; and of professionals from bachelor through master, sixth-year, and doctoral levels.

In overview, this is my idea of the unity concept. It encompasses the generic book, in all of its subjects, levels, and formats. Administratively, the concept does not do away with the library; instead, it reinforces it by making of it a media center. The unity concept adds some new dimensions to the crusade for articulation in education and practice through a renaissance in individual independence.

Philosophically, I believe the unity concept of media is an approach to a truly liberal world mind.

PART I:

THE GENERIC BOOK

HOW TO TAILOR LEARNING

The Florida concept of media education developed since 1947, which led to the national AASL-DAVI Media Standards, was first described here. That concept is expressed as a "faith in the essentiality of instructional materials . . . the connecting link between teacher and pupil, the basic means through which the teacher can tailor learning to meet the individual differences of children."

In the area of instructional materials it can truly be said that the eyes of the educational world are on Florida. Since 1947, librarians, audiovisualists, and textbook managers, as well as many classroom teachers, supervisors, principals, and college professors, have been developing a concept which may have profound implications for the perennial classroom problem of individual differences. In three words, this concept may be called "Unity of Materials."

In a few more words, the concept includes a faith in the essentiality of instructional materials as the connecting link between teacher and pupil, the basic means *through which the teacher can tailor learning to meet the individual differences of children.* To accomplish such tailored learning the classroom teachers and pupils must have free and unhampered access to the whole range of instructional materials—textbooks, library books, 16mm films, and some 37 other classes of instructional materials, examples of which are found in most Florida schools.

The Florida concept starts with the assumption that there is a single universe of instructional materials, not a trichotomy of textbook, library, and audiovisual kingdoms. It contends further that the existence of a separate library, AV center, and textbook depository in the schools is educationally confusing, administratively unsound, and financially uneconomical. Out of these assumptions has come the unity concept of instructional materials.

From these assumptions have emerged the Florida materials centers in individual schools and the county integrated materials program. Although at first glance these new materials centers would appear to be a cross between conventional separate library and separate audiovisual services with increasing relation to the textbook dissemination problem, the fact is that the stronger materials centers are assuming an educational role never before approached by the components separately. In short, by erasing the artificial boundaries among the textbook, library, and audiovisual kingdoms, the new materials centers are providing so exciting a stimulus to teachers and pupils to overcome the obstacle of individual differences that in one master stroke the schools may answer effectively the critics of mass education.

There are now in Florida at least six county school systems with an integrated instructional materials program. In addition, there are an increasing number of elementary and secondary schools all over the state that have replaced their school libraries with materials centers. But what is most significant is the number of classroom teachers in Florida who have caught

Reprinted with permission from the *Journal of the Florida Education Association,* 32:12-13ff. (November 1954).

the potential of integrated instructional materials, as well as librarians, audiovisualists, textbook managers, general supervisors, and principals. This has in no small measure been due to the leadership given this movement by the institutions of higher education in Florida and by the State Department of Education.

Since present certification went into effect, every elementary teacher in Florida has had (under "Plan Two, Area 1") a course entitled "Introduction to Materials for Use with Children." This course covers "familiarity with textbooks, library materials, literature for children, visual aids, etc."[1] Although no comparable certification requirement is indicated for secondary teachers, many high school teachers have elected instructional materials courses in their pre-service education.

What is even more significant is the amount of in-service education in instructional materials that has been going on in Florida since 1947. Through the General Extension Division the state universities have offered basic courses in instructional materials to teachers in their home centers. All of the institutions of higher education in Florida that have summer sessions have, through courses, institutes, conferences, clinics, and workshops, provided instruction to teachers on their campuses in the use of instructional materials.

In 1947 the Board of Control authorized the establishment at Florida State University of a full professional school for the training of librarians of all kinds of libraries. This school is today the only nationally accredited school within a radius of 500 miles from Florida's center. Despite a professional obligation to train librarians for all kinds of libraries—college, public, government, industrial, military, as well as school—and for the nation as well as for Florida, the FSU Library School placed preparation of teachers in the area of instructional materials high in its professional priorities.

In the very first summer of its existence, the concept of unity of materials was introduced in the Leadership Training Work Conference. Amo DeBernardis, then audiovisual supervisor in the Portland, Oregon, schools, served as consultant. The following year the Jacksonville *Times-Union* editorialized on the FSU Library School's vision in activating an audiovisual department headed by Dr. Charles Hoban.

From the start, the FSU Library School made history for the professional education of librarians by adding a required audiovisual course, and an increasing number of audiovisual electives for specialization. Audio-visual units were incorporated in the conventional print material courses universally taken by librarians. Since its activation, the FSU Library School has qualified 335 school and county leaders in librarianship, audiovisual, and instructional materials. During the FSU summer sessions since 1947, no fewer than 3,366 students have enrolled in library and audiovisual courses. And in the school years since 1948, no fewer than 2,053 classroom teachers have taken advantage of library and audiovisual courses offered by the FSU Library School through the General Extension Division in 29 Florida centers extending from Pensacola to Key West.

Add to this record the courses taken in instructional materials in the other Florida institutions of higher education, and it can easily be seen why Florida is better prepared than almost any other state in the union for doing something significant in the area of instructional materials. True, Florida is nowhere near the top in the amount of money it spends per capita for school libraries, for 16mm films, and for the administration of materials programs. This is to be regretted, but it is not to be accepted as an index of achievement in the area of instructional materials.

Other states have had the experience of splurging in 16mm films before classroom teachers and supervisors were ready. The result was an inevitable setback to the whole program. Still other states have suffered from the rivalries inherent in a trichotomy where the sponsors of each kingdom of materials fought the others so enthusiastically as to retard the entire multi-materials concept. Florida has been most fortunate in the fact that from the start a majority of those who work in the area of instructional materials has seen the wisdom of unity.

Florida certification in this area has reflected an evolutionary advance toward this concept. Although No. 18 among Certification Requirements is still headed "Library Service," the specifications encourage inclusion of "books and related materials," a separate two-semester-hour course in audiovisual, and up to 12 additional semester-hours of audiovisual in the elective portion of the requirements, so that a total of 14 semester-hours of the 30 required for certification may be taken in audiovisual, in addition to the audiovisual units that now permeate the basic courses.

Nevertheless, the time has come for the next step in the evolution of certification in this area. Over a period of two years, librarians, audiovisualists, materials specialists, and others interested in this area have been meeting informally as well as in seminars, workshops, and conferences. A state-wide committee has been engaged in an inventory of instructional materials in Florida schools. The FEA Audiovisual and Library Sections have appointed a joint committee to study the possibility of consolidating the two groups into a strong, unified Instructional Materials Section. Out of all these meetings, certain principles for the revision of No. 18 in Florida Certification have been developed.

At an informal meeting in Gainesville, April 4, 1954, an *ad hoc* committee of five[2] Florida specialists in instructional materials drafted a proposed revision of No. 18. Basically, this draft suggests three levels of preparation in instructional materials: 1) for *all* classroom teachers, secondary as well as elementary; 2) for building coordinators at the school level; and 3) for county supervisors.

For classroom teachers, the report of the *ad hoc* committee of five recommends an introductory course in instructional materials for all teachers, secondary as well as elementary.

For building coordinators, the report recommends that the present heading for No. 18, "Library Service," be replaced by the Florida term "Instructional Materials." Three classes of certification are suggested to replace the present two (which, after September 1, 1954, became one):

Certification C. 9 semester-hours required to qualify for service in small schools or as assistant in very large schools, distributed:
(Course 1)
        3 semester-hours. Introduction to Instructional Materials (same as requirement for classroom teachers)

(Course 2)
>3 semester-hours. Supervision of Materials Program

(Course 3)
>3 semester-hours. Principles and Philosophy of Audiovisual

Certification B. 15 semester-hours required to qualify for medium-sized schools to 500 enrollment. In addition to courses 1, 2, and 3:

(Course 4)
>3 semester-hours. Organization and Administration of Instructional Materials

(Course 5)
>3 semester hours. Selection and Utilization of Instructional Materials

Certification A. 20 semester-hours required to qualify for large schools. In addition to courses 1 through 5, any five semester-hours chosen from the following:

(Course 6)
>2 semester-hours. Classification and Cataloging

(Course 7)
>3 semester hours. Reference Materials and Services

(Course 8)
>3 semester-hours. Production of Audiovisual Materials

(Course 9)
>3 semester-hours. Advanced Selection and Use of Instructional Materials

For county supervisors of instructional materials, the *ad hoc* committee recommended that certification should parallel certification requirements for special supervisors, and strongly urged a master's degree and at least five years of successful teaching experience. Professional training should include at least 30 semester-hours, distributed:

>15 semester-hours from Certification A
>6 semester-hours in AV, at least three of which should be in production
>3 semester-hours in Curriculum
>3 semester-hours in Supervision

The committee presented its report to a special pre-convention meeting called jointly by the chairmen of the FEA Audiovisual and Library Sections in Miami on April 7, 1954. Over 100 librarians, audiovisualists and other FEA members attended this two-hour session. At the conclusion those in attendance voted in favor of the following amendments to the report:

1. That the term "instructional materials" replace both "library" and "audiovisual."
2. That the course "Principles and Philosophy" encompass the whole range of instructional materials rather than just audiovisual.
3. That the course titled "Supervision of Materials Program" be retitled "Organization and Administration of Materials Program," and that a course in general supervision not be considered equivalent.

Amendments favored by a majority but on which some differences still exist related to "C" certification. Many believe there should be just two certifications, "B" and "A." Other differences that were marked were those relating to the basic course in classification and cataloging, which some thought should be required in the minimum certificate and increased to three semester-hours.

The consensus of the meeting appeared to consider the report of the *ad hoc* committee a basis for revising certification and favored refining it so as to reconcile the five specific differences that developed in the discussion.

In view of the fact that "Restricted Certification" has now been removed from No. 18 of Certification, and considering the sentiment of the integrated concept, it would seem highly desirable to proceed with moderate haste to the revision of certification in this area. Consummation of this revision and conclusion of the materials inventory provide Florida with the basis for moving forward to a point of national leadership in this educational area.

FOOTNOTES

1. *Florida Requirements for Teacher Education and Certification*, adopted April 3, 1951; revised and adopted July 21, 1953. p. 257.

2. Charles Cates, University of Florida; Robert Clapp, Florida State University; Edgar Lane, Dade County Schools; Hazel Morgan, General Extension Division; Louis Shores, Florida State University.

UNION NOW: THE AV WAY AND THE LIBRARY WAY

The media dichotomy promoted by some militant librarians and audiovisualists in the post-World War II years resulted in what was probably this first dialogue between me and Professor Ole Larson of Indiana University. It was a gracious exchange between us as we agreed in correspondence to undertake a definition of the two positions: separate audiovisual and library centers, or unified materials centers. Because the late Paul Reed, editor of Educational Screen, understood the issue so well and was so receptive to my proposal that Professor Larson and I undertake this dialogue, I have also reprinted Mr. Reed's introduction.

THIS IS PART ONE

The falseness of the supposed battle between books and films we have pointed out many times in the pages of *Educational Screen* (most recently in our editorial, "Who's Scaring the Librarians?," January, 1955 issue). Equally exaggerated is the notion that across the country librarians and audiovisual people are at one another's throats, fighting for separate identity, self-determination, self-interest.

There *is*, however, plenty of genuine and sincere disagreement about the wisdom or lack of wisdom in merging the library way and the audiovisual way into one way. In Florida the union is already well developed. In other places there is some degree of coordination. In other places the audiovisual way and the library way are distinctly separate ways.

Because of the importance of this difference of opinion and development, *Educational Screen* has asked a well-known and respected proponent of each "side" to present his point of view. This month Louis Shores (Dean, Library School, Florida State University, Tallahassee) gives you the "Unity of Materials" point of view. He explains how and why in Florida audiovisualists and librarians have agreed to unite the audiovisual way with the library way. In a later issue, you will read another point of view, to be presented by L. C. Larson (Director, Audio-Visual Center, Indiana University, Bloomington).

As is often the case, we suspect the two points of view are not as far apart as they may appear to some. We suspect, too, there are other points of view.

And now we invite you to read carefully the case for the "Unity of Materials." We also invite your reactions.

Editor's Note

The audiovisual movement in American education is today at the crossroads. It can continue along its separate way sponsoring only those teaching media that employ a maximum of concrete and a minimum of verbal experiences. Or it can embrace the entire range of instructional materials found in American schools. The issue is as simple as that.

Reprinted with permission from *Educational Screen*, 34:112-15 (March 1955).

Nor can the decision be delayed much longer. The Department of Audiovisual Instruction recently issued to its members the "Report on Exploratory Conference on Certification of Audiovisual Instructional Materials Supervisors." Both the conference and the report are most timely, and the DAVI Board of Directors is to be congratulated on its foresight.

But the report as it now reads leaves the impression that the exploration is to be segmentary. Since the present report is restricted to certification of *audiovisual* instructional materials supervisors only, state certification agencies will expect explorations of certification for other instructional materials supervisors, those that supervise textbook, library, and even newer categories of teaching media now seeking separate recognition. There is inherent in this piecemeal consideration of the certification problem a promise that at some point in these preliminary explorations these segments will be related to each other and the resulting instructional materials arc fitted into the circle of professional licensing.

Since similar explorations have been under way for some time in various states and since, as the report points out, any national conclusions will have to be followed by activities "on the state level to secure adoption of desirable certification requirements," a first step would appear to be an inventory of present teacher certification requirements in the 48 states. This review should focus attention on every possible point in the present teacher certification code of a state that relates or might possibly relate to strengthening the qualifications of educational personnel in the area of instructional materials. As a contribution to this first step, there is presented here the experience of one state.

In many ways, Florida certification in this area has been unique. To those inside the state, and to a growing number outside who really understand what has been going on during the last seven years, the Florida plan holds great promise for a certification pattern that may find at long last the rightful place in our schools not only for audiovisual but for all kinds of instructional materials.

Since 1947, audiovisualists, librarians, and textbook managers, on the one hand, and interested classroom teachers, principals, and college professors, on the other, have been developing together a concept which may have profound implications for the perennial problem of classroom differences. In three words, this concept may be called "unity of materials." In a few more words, it may be described as a basic faith in the essentiality of instructional materials; a conviction that, as important as the learner and the teacher are in the learning process, their efforts are almost entirely dependent upon the medium of communication between them. Now while these media may take many forms and formats, there is a basic unity among all of them. Their purpose is the same—to link teacher and learner, communicant and communicand, in such a way as to achieve education.

The Florida concept starts, therefore, with the assumption that there is one world of instructional materials, not a trichotomy of audiovisual, library, and textbook kingdoms. It contends that separate audiovisual, library, and textbook centers in the school are educationally confusing to the ultimate consumer, administratively unsound, and financially uneconomical. Out of these assumptions has come the concept of unity of materials. From these contentions there is evolving in Florida a pattern of Instructional Materials Certification that seeks to reconcile not only such segmentary licensing as occurs in this area but the transitional compromises, necessitated by present limitations, with the ultimate objective, which wisdom dictates should be attempted only in evolutionary stages.

To translate this concept into happenings, Florida is experiencing a metamorphosis of its school libraries, audiovisual centers, and textbook depositories. Its emerging materials centers are much more than a merging of all three. Startlingly, something entirely different from any one of them is even now beginning to peek out of the conventional cocoons still found in many of our schools.

And if that is happening to the materials centers, even more marked changes are occurring in the personnel who supervise, administer, and use these centers. As a new generation of pupils, classroom teachers, coordinators, and supervisors emerges, county by county, it is evident how wrong those people are who jump to hasty conclusions about the Florida concept. For, lo and behold, the supervisor is neither an audiovisualist nor a librarian, but truly a supervisor of instructional materials, dealing with all 40 forms and formats, ranging from textbooks to television through magazines and motion pictures, over field trips and filmstrips, across radio and recordings, with pictures and peepboxes, and on and on. All of this one must comprehend more fully if one is to understand the developing pattern of Florida instructional materials certification.

Against this brief background, present Florida certification in the area of instructional materials must be considered as representing only a stage along the route. As the Florida pattern now stands, on the eve of another probable major revision, it begins with the classroom teacher. It specifies that every elementary teacher in Florida, to be licensed, must have a course in "Introduction to Materials for Use with Children," which includes familiarity with textbooks, library materials, literature for children, visual aids, etc. Although no comparable requirement is indicated at present in the certification of secondary teachers, it is notable that an increasing number of high school teachers have elected work in this area and that one of the major proposed changes is that the same requirement of competence in instructional materials be included across the board for all classroom teachers.

From the *classroom* teacher, Florida certification in instructional materials proceeds to the certification of the *school* teacher who is to serve as the instructional materials leader, or controller, or coordinator for the building. This individual may be an audiovisualist, a librarian, a textbook manager, or a classroom teacher with some other specialty. His primary interest may be in motion pictures, children's books, educational television, bulletin boards, or any one of a score or more categories of instructional materials. However, he must have a belief in and an enthusiasm for the mission of instructional materials and he must meet minimum certification requirements.

What are these minimum certification requirements? In view of the quotes and misquotes about Florida certification in the instructional materials area attributed to some audiovisualists, it is well to set down here first what is actually on the books now, before indicating the work on the new revision proposed for this year.

In the "Florida Requirements for Teacher Education and Certification," last revised and adopted July 21, 1953, the first point that stands out in certification of instructional materials personnel on the school level is the teacher education prerequisite. This says, in effect, that the candidate for licensing must present as part of the bachelor's degree: 1) approximately two college years of general education, 2) the teacher certification requirement of general professional education, and 3) the teacher certification requirement of one or more areas of specialized professional education, such as art, music, English, science, social studies, etc.

The second significant point is that instructional materials has been recognized as one of the specialized professional education areas. Among the numbered specialized areas in Florida certification, instructional materials is No. 18. On the teacher certification base it specifies two certifications: 1) *Restricted*, for coordinators in schools with enrollment up to 300; and 2) *Full*, for coordinators in schools with enrollment over 300.

Restricted certification in instructional materials specifies 12 semester hours of courses in the area of instructional materials. The four three-semester-hour courses are as follows:

1) *Introduction to Materials*. This is the course that also meets the requirement in the certification of elementary classroom teachers and that is being strongly urged as a requirement in the certification of secondary teachers as well. As its title suggests, this is an overview of the principal classes of instructional materials found in Florida schools, with special emphasis on children's books and their illustration, textbooks, school recordings, selected films, filmstrips, pictures, bulletin boards, etc., their use (or utilization, depending upon which group of terminologists you belong to), selection, sources for review, grading, and evaluation.

2) *Organization and Administration of a School Materials Center*. Here is the first course aimed directly at the teacher who has become enthusiastic enough about the potential for learning in multiple-materials to want to learn something about running a school program. In this course acquisition techniques for acquiring all kinds of instructional materials are taught, including sources, prices, discounts, order forms, etc. Here, also, methods of classifying, indexing, and maintaining them are considered. Considerable attention is given to circulating and disseminating these materials so that they will enter the mainstream of the school's learning program. The mechanics of charging, booking and otherwise lending, keeping records, mending, labeling, splicing, and other techniques are demonstrated.

3) *Curriculum Materials*. This is a sequel to course number one. It aims to study the evaluation, selection, and use of more school materials, but this time even more closely related to the specific school areas of the language arts, social studies, science, fine and industrial arts, etc.

4) *Foundations or Principles of an Instructional Materials Program*. This is a philosophy course, but it is also much more. Here the multi-material concept in the learning process can be introduced and traced through the major historical impetuses of the printing press, the textbook, school libraries, and audiovisual centers to the emerging materials centers and the growing acceptance of unity.

These, then, are the four course requirements for the so-called "restricted" certificate in the area of instructional materials. Notable is the fact that the first of these four courses is the one required for the certification of all elementary classroom teachers and urged for the certification of all secondary teachers. Equally important is the fact that this course is articulated with the succeeding three so that the materials-minded classroom teacher can progressively prepare for increasing instructional materials opportunities and responsibilities in her school.

Full certification in instructional materials likewise articulates with what has gone before. To the 12 semester hours required for restricted certification are added 18 additional semester hours, for a total of 30. The distribution of these additional 18 semester hours specifies three two-semester-hour courses, two of which give advanced attention to two special classes of instructional materials, and the third to more detailed problems of organizing materials collections in larger schools and in county centers. Of the first two, one course is devoted to school reference materials and sources for locating information about all of the classes of materials; the other course, called Audiovisual Materials, stimulates the production of inexpensive school-made materials as well as further study of the use of films, filmstrips, recordings, flat pictures, and some other classes of instructional materials.

The remaining 12 hours in the 30-hour instructional materials specialization may be selected from advanced courses in audiovisual production and use, in reading, in children's literature, etc.

From school coordinator to county supervisor, certification is only implied by the general paragraph which now covers licensing of all special supervisors. Applying these general provisions to the instructional materials area, there is now indicated 1) a specialization such as has been described for school coordinator certification; 2) a master's degree, and 3) a minimum of three years of successful school experience.

This is Florida certification in instructional materials, as of this school year of 1954-55, with one exception. Beginning September 1, 1954, "restricted" certificate has been removed. For the concerned audiovisualist, it is also important to note that No. 18 in Florida Certification is still headed "Library Service." The reasons for that are not hard to understand if the evolution of certification in this area is understood. Schools seek regional as well as state accreditation. Until the past year Florida's No. 18 had to comply with the specifications of the Southern Association of Colleges and Secondary Schools. Further, regardless of the fact that labels are more important psychologically than rationally, the fact remains that no better term than librarian has yet been agreed upon for the school coordinator's title.

Nearly every summer in the Florida State University Summer School, groups of instructional materials majors in the Library School discuss this problem of a name. At one of these meetings, the writer suggested jestingly that since we deal with materials, we call ourselves "materialists." It was objected that the present salary level did not justify such a title. Moving then to the other extreme, it was suggested that since we deal with media of communications, we call ourselves "mediums"! The importance and difficulty of selecting a label have undoubtedly also contributed to the persistence of the "library" designation.

But aside from the label, the content of the specialized area and its implication for the audiovisual movement are inescapable. The basic 12 semester hours of courses cover instructional materials of all types, including considerable attention to those most often labelled audiovisual. Of the remaining 18 hours, as many as 14 may be taken in specialized audiovisual courses.

The question might now be asked, how has this certification helped instructional materials in Florida schools? It cannot be claimed that Florida spends as much per pupil on textbooks, library materials, and audiovisual materials as some other states do, although progress is evident in the last few years. But it can be claimed that in no state has there been a greater increase quantitatively and qualitatively of competent personnel in the whole range of instructional materials.

For example, in seven years, Florida State University alone has qualified 335 leaders in the instructional materials field who are serving as county supervisors, audiovisualists, librarians and materials specialists. Two are serving as state supervisors. During the eight summer sessions alone, no fewer than 3,366 students, for the most part Florida teachers, have enrolled in instructional materials courses. During the seven school years in between, extension courses in instructional materials have been brought to no fewer than 2,053 classroom teachers in their home communities in some 29 Florida centers extending from Pensacola to Key West.

The impact of this educational program is evident at a number of points in Florida education. At least seven counties now have a supervisor of instructional materials. In school after school, the old-fashioned audiovisual centers and school libraries are giving way to the new materials centers. The individuals who coordinate these school centers think of themselves less and less as librarians or audiovisualists, and more and more as instructional materials leaders. Some of them began as audiovisualists; some of them began as librarians; but most of them started as classroom teachers. Regardless of their professional origins, there is a solidarity among those who work with instructional materials that is immediately marked by visiting speakers at state meetings.

In the last two years the instructional materials leaders in Florida have been concerned with two major projects: 1) an inventory of instructional materials in Florida schools, and 2) the revision of certification. The former is nearing publication stage; the latter has now entered an advanced exploratory conference, under the direction of the state Teacher Education Advisory Council, whose recommendations on certification are usually tantamount to adoption.

Among the documents the Council will have under consideration is a draft of a proposed revision of No. 18 prepared by an *ad hoc* committee of five materials specialists and the crystallization of some agreements and differences on certification revision brought out in a joint meeting of the library and audiovisual sections of the Florida Education Association held in Miami last April. Because these points of agreement and difference are basic to any exploration of certification in the instructional materials area, they are here summarized. First, the points of agreement:

1) The term "instructional materials" should replace both of the terms "library" and "audiovisual" in certification.

2) The specialized course in "Principles and Philosophy" should encompass the whole range of instructional materials rather than just "library materials" or "audiovisual" materials separately.

3) The basic or first course in instructional materials should be a requirement for certification of all classroom teachers, secondary as well as elementary.

4) Specialization for instructional materials leadership on the school level should be based on teacher certification and should lead to at least two levels of competence: a) basic, for minimum competence in any school, and b) advanced competence for extended responsibility.

5) Specialization for instructional materials leadership on the county level (there are no city school systems in Florida though similar competence might be expected in the states where there are) should be based on teacher certification, a master's degree, at least five years of successful school experience, and a 30-semester-hour graduate professional program at least half of which would have been accomplished in instructional materials courses with at least six semester hours in curriculum development and in supervision.

Differences developed around details. One group favored three, rather than two, levels of certification for competence on the school level. Another group felt there should be more emphasis on a separate course in classification and cataloging of instructional materials and that it should be required in the lowest level of certification.

From these agreements and differences it is at least evident that Florida has left the crossroads. For better or for worse, audiovisualists and librarians have agreed to unite the audiovisual way with the library way.

LIBRARY AND AV CENTER–COMBINED OR SEPARATE?

Opinions still differed in 1958. At the invitation of the editor of the official journal of the National Education Association, I undertook to state the issue and present the case for unity in a forum with two school superintendents: Harold Spears of San Francisco, and James W. Bushong of Grosse Pointe, Michigan. Added is the journal's abridged form of "Prerequisites" for instructional materials specialists developed by a Joint Committee of AASL, ACRL, and DAVI.

Some schools have a school library and a separate audiovisual center. Other schools place all instructional materials and equipment in one place, which is called either a school library or a materials center.

Advocates of dual centers contend that there is a difference between library materials and audiovisual materials, that librarians and audiovisualists differ in their educational concept and technical procedures. For these reasons, separatists argue that every school should have separate audiovisual and library centers, or at least should have different people administering them.

There are separatists among both librarians and audiovisualists. Some librarians say they already have their hands full caring for printed materials and cannot take on the additional responsibility of films, filmstrips, and the equipment necessary to project them. Some audiovisualists support this position and say that librarians and audiovisualists should cooperate but should not integrate their services.

Advocates of the single center, however, who include many librarians, audiovisualists, and a new generation of instructional materials specialists, believe that teachers and pupils are best served by a single resource center in the school and by a unified, integrated instructional materials program in the school system.

The integrationist sees any separation of audiovisual and library materials and services as artificial, costly, and confusing to teachers and pupils. He believes that dual materials centers in the long run reduce the effective use of school materials.

From the professional literature of both librarianship and audiovisual instruction, it is almost impossible to determine where library materials leave off and audiovisual materials begin. The following classes of school materials are claimed by both librarians and audiovisualists: maps, globes, charts, pictures, bulletin boards, exhibits, discs, and tape recordings.

Consequently, in a school with dual centers, there must be a division of spoils between the audiovisual center and the school library. In one school, for example, maps and globes are housed in the library and charged to the audiovisual center's budget. This confronts both teachers and pupils with the necessity of having to decide which center to go to for the specific materials they need.

Reprinted with permission from *Today's Education: NEA Journal*, 47:342-44 (May, 1958).

Nor is the line clear-cut on books and films. Some school libraries house, catalog, and classify filmstrips. Some even rent films. Because of the interrelationships among all school materials, the integrationist advocates housing the full range of instructional materials in a single resource center.

Part of the separatist's argument is that the combined job is too much for one person. The integrationist sees this argument as illogical.

In some small schools with separate audiovisual and library centers, there are part-time teacher-librarians who devote half-time to teaching and half-time to administering the library. Another teacher is relieved part-time to administer the audiovisual service. The integrationist believes the school program would be better served by a full-time librarian who would administer a unified materials center that would procure, house, classify, catalog, disseminate, and guide the use of the whole range of instructional materials.

In the larger schools with dual centers, there is usually at least one full-time librarian and one audiovisual coordinator operating separate centers. The integrationist advocates combining the two centers by providing:

1) A single catalog of all of the school's instructional materials, so that at a glance teachers and pupils can discover what resources are available on a topic—books, films, periodicals, filmstrips, discs, pictures, tapes, objects, an index of community resources;

2) A single charging and booking system for all of these classes of materials;

3) A unified guidance and reference service for pupils and teachers—organized judiciously by levels or subjects if necessary.

The integrationist believes that when two people are assigned to guide the use of instructional materials in the school, they would be most effective in a single center, dividing the work between them—if such division is desirable—not by type of materials, but by level or subject specialization.

In a high school, for example, the integrationist feels that one materials specialist might perhaps serve the sciences and industrial arts; the other, the language arts and social studies. He believes these people would serve learning more effectively by becoming specialists in levels or subjects rather than in a particular area of materials.

On the other hand, the separatist argues that education is best served by having one specialist handle audiovisual materials and equipment and the other handle library materials—usually in two different places in the building.

Here is an issue that is clear-cut. In the years ahead, universal education will increase the range of individual differences. This will make it necessary to have more and varied instructional materials, expertly adapted to pupil learning requirements. How to organize the school's instructional materials program must be decided now. It seems to me that a unified materials center in the school is clearly supported by trends and logic.

REACTIONS

I. By Harold Spears, Superintendent of Schools, San Francisco, California

A separate library and a separate audiovisual center or one unified instructional materials center? The administrators of each school district are responsible for deciding which method seems logical for their particular situation. Naturally, this decision can best be reached after proper study and consultation, with full participation of interested parties. A few road signs seem apparent for those seeking a good instructional materials setup:

Efficiency of school operation invites just one instructional materials center. Such a plan is not only financially sound but saves wear and tear on both teachers and students who avail themselves of such instructional services.

On the other hand, any concept of school organizational setup, such as the one under consideration, is conditioned by the personnel involved. A unified center, although practical in the idea stage, may not be so in practice if the action brings with it personnel problems due either to lack of ability or to poor staff morale. Timing is an essential aspect of change in school operational procedures.

Large high schools had libraries before they had centers for audiovisual materials, librarians before they had audiovisual personnel. In most instances, such schools still have more personnel for the former service than for the latter.

Consequently, the librarians as a group are in the saddle with respect to leading the way to the proper road ahead. If they see the possibilities of the combined center and want to assume responsibility for it, they could get it in most instances by indicating to their adminstrators that they were interested in expanding their operation. Any inclination to shy away from the added responsibilities might be lessened by the anticipation of the eventual upgrading of their positions.

Inadequate preparation for such responsibilities might be overcome to an extent by advanced summer or evening courses or by other individual endeavor. Furthermore, other personnel might well be involved that would enable a good manager to supplement his own skills and abilities with those of others.

The eventual decision in any school should reflect what is best for the education of the student. Those who seek the right answer to this issue are more likely to find it if they start with this premise.

II. By James B. Bushong, Superintendent of Schools, Grosse Pointe, Michigan

Our major emphasis in Grosse Pointe public schools is directed toward the total effect of plans, personnel, and materials on the classroom youngster. Let's keep this emphasis in mind as we consider the proposal to unite the work of the instructional materials specialist with that of the school librarian.

A true specialist in instructional materials must be a first-rate educator. He must have proved his skill in the classroom, have shown imagination, have given evidence of professional fire. He needs to be acquainted with curriculum planning, administration, supervision, research, and methodology. Finally, he must really want to do this particular kind of educational service.

The dedicated librarian must also be a master teacher. He must have many of the skills and much of the knowledge listed above. He must want to encourage reading, promote great ideas, stimulate young minds, satisfy curiosity. He must be sold on what he is attempting to do for boys and girls and for teachers. He must want to perform these functions before all others.

The audiovisual specialist and the librarian—each position requires different preparation and qualifications. I know there must be some individuals who are able to encompass these two vast areas of specialization. Yet, to do both well? How many are so endowed? I believe it's unwise to lump the lot together. Surely whatever might be gained administratively by this expedient would be offset by a weakening of educational benefits.

In Grosse Pointe, we practice cooperative separateness. In every school, there are a librarian and an audiovisual specialist who cooperatively complement each other's services. Each of these specialists, together with his materials and the organization by which his service is performed, is under the wing of our department of instruction.

Our school librarians seem happy to leave the audiovisual materials to the coordinators. They feel the use of maps and globes, small museum pieces, record players, tape recorders, prints, slides, films, projectors, screens, and kindred supplements is better left in the competent hands of carefully trained technicians.

On the other hand, the AV specialists have expressed satisfaction with our method of leaving to competent librarians the responsibility for books, lists, supplements, magazines, pamphlets, and similar materials. This dual system enables each specialist to master his own province, offer highly skilled service, perform a unique function. Thus, each is happy doing what comes naturally—to him. From what we've seen of this program in action, it seems to suit our needs admirably. Therefore, until better arguments are advanced for changing, we will continue to practice cooperative separateness.

THE UNITY OF MATERIALS

Britain, stirred by my crusade for library recognition of audio-visualism, published in the August Librarian *a lengthy excerpt, with a concluding commentary: "This statement of Louis Shores is irrefutable. The time is long past that we can tolerate the three kingdoms of Textbooks, Library Print, and Audio-Visual. Each librarian must do his bit to bridge the schism. . . ."*

My fellow librarians, greetings to you in California from us in Florida. It was my keenest desire to be with you, for what you are doing in this workshop is of utmost importance to all of us in librarianship. The profession owes a very large debt to librarians like Miss Rufsvold, Mr. Lieberman, and Mr. Swank and the members of the Audio-Visual Committee, who have kept our responsibility for media other than print constantly before us. Since I cannot be with you in person I have selected to transmit to you, through one of the newer media, part of the message I have been sending to my students and colleagues ever since 1934 when we began our first AV program at Peabody.

It begins with Mark Hopkins, the pupil and the log—the three symbolic elements of the learning process. Because much has been written about both the teacher's and the pupil's parts in education, nothing about these two is added here. But the log between the teacher and a pupil, which I accept as the symbol of the medium of communication between them, interests me. Now, this log represents all the materials of communication that the teacher uses with the pupil in this life process we call education. If we look at the world of materials available to the teacher today, we see that in most American schools it is divided into three kingdoms—I won't say empires. One of these is the Kingdom of Textbooks, another is the Kingdom of Library Print, and a third is the Kingdom of Audiovisual. All three of these kingdoms are, of course, in continuous danger of subdivision. The textbook faces the threat of separation from the workbook. Library print readily is divided into reference books, serials, government publications, and various subject areas. If audiovisual is not careful, it may one day become a subdivision of television; but for the moment in most of our schools, these are the three monarchies of TB, LP, and AV. All three are part of the log. The three kingdoms comprise the world of materials at the disposal of the teacher and pupil as together they promote the learning process on which mankind must depend for survival. To do an effective job of learning, teacher and pupil must be able to cut across the boundary lines of these three kingdoms completely. As every learning situation has its own peculiar demands, so does every learner. Because if individual difference means anything at all as an educational term, it means that almost no two of us have exactly the same cultural support for the learning we are undertaking. And this means the log between teacher and pupil must be individually tailored—bespoke, as our British friends would say. Only freedom of movement in the whole world of materials, regardless of the

Reprinted from the transcript of a tape prepared for the Los Angeles pre-ALA Audio-Visual Workshop, June 21, 1953, as it was subsequently published in the *Proceedings*, edited by Irving Lieberman.

form of the individual medium, can provide an adequate climate for the learning process.

Now, if we look at the three kingdoms of materials we find the boundary lines as artificial as many of our political ones. What is a flat picture, for example? If it appears in a textbook, it is of course in the TB Kingdom. If it appears in a reference book, it is in the LP Kingdom. And if it appears by itself, it belongs in the AV Kingdom. The same is true of maps. Nor is presence or absence of verbalism a factor. Picture textbooks and picture reference books without one line of text are not placed in the AV Kingdom, nor is the soundfilm or radio transcription full of words accepted in some TB or LP Kingdoms. The distinctions among the three kingdoms are therefore highly arbitrary. Because we as librarians did not see this unity of materials of the media of communication early or universally enough, a bad schism has developed. Those working with textbooks early separated themselves and developed defenses against the use of multiple materials. In turn, some librarians began to look with concern toward the inroads made into reading time by film, radio, and TV. The result was the appearance of three groups of materials' workers in our school systems—textbook directors, librarians, and audiovisualists—all competing for school dollars.

In Florida, we have moved to remedy these differences. From the start, the Library School of Florida State University dedicated itself to the concept of the unity of materials. It did so in its curriculum and it did so in the services which it undertook to operate as a demonstration of this concept. In 1947 it established a materials center for acquiring, processing, and disseminating representative examples of materials in all three kingdoms. It further developed a catalog which interfiled cards describing all types of media. Through a quarterly bulletin called *Materials*, the Library School sought to disseminate information about all the materials of instruction— textbook, library, and audiovisual. In 1947 an audiovisual service was also established. It undertook to provide films, filmstrips, tape and disc recordings, flat pictures, charts, and graphics of various kinds to support university instruction. This audiovisual service went further and set up a film rental library for schools and libraries in Florida. Now it may be questioned whether a Library School should operate such extensive services. We ourselves question it and believe perhaps ultimately that the University Library should operate them for our instruction and for our institution. But we needed a demonstration of what we were teaching and, since none was available, we created it. Last year a very important step was taken in Florida. The State Superintendent of Instruction appointed a statewide Commission on Instructional Materials. On that Commission are audiovisualists, textbook directors, and librarians. We held a workshop in our Library School last spring. Out of that workshop has come an integrated instrument now being refined for measuring materials services in the schools of Florida. Out of that workshop has come also the embryo curriculum for educating a new generation of librarians who will perform their functions *not by books alone*.

At this point we are uncertain what to call these new librarians. Here we are in Florida today with an augmented professional concept but without a name. If you can think of an adequate one, I hope you will send us that name for our use. Despite the audiovisualists', librarians', and textbook directors' previous fears of each other, we have come together in Florida. We have a unified materials front. We have become articulate enough to earn legislative action. Librarians can accomplish this everywhere. All we need to do is overcome some of the diffidence we have about machinery and some of the defense we have developed against the newer media.

Let me recall to you that provocative book by Georges Duhamel, *In Defense of Letters*, which appeared during the year of the outbreak of World War II. I quote:

> Various indications lead us to suppose that books—the essential diet of the elect, the master minds—are going to play an ever-diminishing role in the enlightenment and entertainment of the multitude. Even though the statisticians try to prove with the aid of figures that the output of books is going ahead normally, I am still unable to suppress my anxiety. People who follow the march of events know that the book trade is in distress. More and more books are being published—I know that well enough. They are the somersaults and convulsions of an industry which is playing all its cards to give itself an illusion of vitality. The decadence of the book, the greatest instrument for the diffusion of knowledge, may be delayed a little longer; on the other hand, it may be precipitated by social upheavals.

These fears of Duhamel are shared by too many of us for the good of our overall cause. I believe Joseph Wood Krutch, eminent critic though he is, has not properly evaluated the relationships of books and non-book materials. The reply that Edgar Dale—who was identified with readability long before it was associated with audiovisualism—offered to Mr. Krutch makes very much sense to me. There will always be a place for the book, but there is also a place for the newer media. The supreme challenge to librarianship is to provide the professional integrating force that will inform every member of society through the most effective medium.

The library today must therefore become the preserver and disseminator of all the records of civilization, regardless of what physical shape or form they may have. It is my hope that you will dedicate yourselves to advancing the cause of all media of communication, so that we as librarians may more effectively serve this troubled world.

OF MEDIA AND MEDIUMS

Since "librarian" is not acceptable as an occupational label to audiovisualists, and since "audiovisualist" will not be adopted by librarians, why not appropriate the common professional designation of "medium." Spiritualists should have no copyright on this term. More significantly, for a new merged association of both groups, a state media program is proposed.

Today's American revolution in education has much cause. But its effect, to date, has been comparatively negative. The campus disorders have been overwhelmingly against, rarely for, an education idea. School strikes have largely, and justly, sought comparatively fairer compensation from a way of life that prides itself on justice. But rarely have protesters advanced a learning innovation.

The fact is that the current learning mode is inadequate for the American dream. Part of that dream, to the consternation of some, is that every American is a potential candidate for higher education. I happen to believe that. As long ago as 1948, I debated elitism with one of Robert Hutchins' disciples. I still believe in college for everyone. But I do not believe in the kind of college we have today for everyone—and this is despite the fact that I have served on an American college faculty for more than four decades.

First, let me say why I believe in college for everyone. If I read my history critically, I come to the conclusion that one cause for violent revolution in the past is the inability of the 10 percent with higher education to communicate with the 90 percent without it. Consequently, I am excited about our American courage in placing a junior college practically within walking distance of the home of every high school graduate in the United States. While many nations of the world are still struggling with illiteracy because of inadequate elementary schools, and most countries still provide too little secondary education, America boldly strides toward college for all. God bless Americans. Perhaps history will not find us as ugly as do contemporary anti-Americans at home and abroad.

But noble as this objective is—to open college doors to all—it will fail ignobly unless we who have devoted our lives to education are willing to reexamine our professional folklore. I challenge us to fight any sense of insecurity in this reexamination. I urge us to attack our Establishment as critically as the demonstrators do, but more intelligently than they have. I am confident that we will at least exercise our heads, rather than our feet, as they do.

As I have declared before, and as Associated Press newspapers have reported with varying degrees of sympathy, the "March" has been an inadequate form of communication. It has accomplished very little that is positive or creative in any of the current causes. This is so because those who resort to physical effort are usually too fatigued, or too incompetent, to think creatively. They are mostly exhibitionists, who have desired but never earned a place on the stage. Their leaders are often demagogues who have

Essay for the first annual meeting of the Nebraska Educational Media Association, a merger of the state school library association and audiovisual association, Cornhusker Hotel, Lincoln, March 14, 1969.

gained less attention than their egos demanded.

This being so, it behooves us who work in education to effect a positive revolution in our schools and colleges, in our libraries, and in other communication agencies. And of all the education groups I know, none has quite the means—strategically or tactically—to bring about the changes needed in our education, that we who work in media have. This includes all of us: those of us who call ourselves librarians; those who insist we are audiovisualists; those who identify as information scientists; journalists of the press and periodicals; communicators through television and radio; and mediums of all kinds of media formats, who have an impact on shaping our national mind, and even more importantly, the world intelligence. I say to you that the success of the educational revolution is in our hands. And I call upon you, my colleagues, to overcome the thoughtless negativism of our current campus unrest.

There is only one way to do this, in my opinion. One must first identify solutions, then identify problems. I know this is revolutionary in itself. The stance of the scientific method, which has dominated all of my approaches since my own Chicago student days in the early 1930s, is the opposite. But our world is now so full of problems that have been identified again and again, and all of us have been depressed by fatigue and futility, beyond the mood for solutions. That is probably why it is so much easier to be against something, and so much more unrewarding to be for something.

At the outset, I recognize these basic, just, causes against our American education, on all levels. Two of the three are the result of growing pains from our courageous attempt to educate everybody. The third is truly due to the Establishment. In order, the just causes for complaint against American education can be identified as 1) growing impersonality; 2) lockstep learning; 3) prescriptive disciplines. These are legitimate causes for intellectual protest, although never for physical violence.

Let me elaborate. Numbers have made our education more impersonal than ever before. Observe the mob scenes in our gymnasia on registration days. If enthusiasm for learning overcomes the opening day frustrations, it has only begun its diversion by irrelevancies to the main business of education. Witness, for example, huge classes in which a prima donna professor gratifies his ego by entering tardily like the conductor of a symphony, and then by dispensing, grandiloquently, facts that any student could acquire more quickly on his own, if he had ever been given the sophisitication to use a library intelligently. Unable to cope with the numbers in his class on a personal basis, the professor resorts to the computer for evaluation of individuals. By means of something called a scientific measuring instrument, the student reveals his character with plus or minus marks; a yes or a no; a preference among four choices. After playing this deadly game the student waits, like a gambler at the roulette wheel, for the computer to pass judgment—not objectively, as the faculty insist, but impersonally, as the student feels.

Despite the fact that the numbers on our campuses and in our schools have introduced the widest range of individual differences that have ever confronted faculties, we continue to group-teach in the classroom. When higher education was restricted to the upper 10 percent, an average class presentation had a better chance of touching everyone. Furthermore, the limited number of books available, and the absence of non-print media, necessitated oral feeding of pupils by the teacher. But the advance of universal education on all levels has steadily rendered the classroom mode of teaching ineffective. Not only are the gifted bored, and the underdeveloped frustrated, but even the center of the statisticians' beloved bell-shaped curve flounders aimlessly around clocked class periods, which become the basic measure of education. It is a lockstep learning that denies the very word "liberal" on which so many academicians pride themselves.

What "impersonality" and "lockstep" leave undiscouraged in the student's initial enthusiasm is frequently finished off by the curriculum. All of us who have given our lives to education are aware that there is a hierarchy of disciplines. Some subjects are more respectable than others. Right now, the natural sciences are riding the roost, with the result that the social sciences, including even history, strive valiantly to operate under the sacred method. "For what else is there?," they ask, mimicking the affluent physical and biological sciences. No one can deny the wonders of air conditioning, the automobile, or space capsules. No wonder that even the humanities have capitulated to science. A novel becomes a bestseller because the novelist has devoted five years to research. The drama glories in "telling it like it is" rather than as it might be. C. P. Snow's two cultures have never more nearly been reduced to one.

As a result, God's universe is presented to the student in separate parts: chemistry from nine to eleven on Monday, Wednesday, Friday; economics from two to four on Tuesday and Thursday; literature at other regular class hours. Although a movement called "general education" has tried valiantly to bring together the separate science segments into an integrated area and to synthesize into "humanities" the various subjects called the arts, language, literature, and philosophy, the effort has not been entirely successful. Powerful forces of specialization enforce allegiances to disciplines; faculty, in turn, compel student acceptance of this segmented approach to a study of the riddle of the universe.

Well, enough about the problems. Now to the solutions, which our demonstrators never seem to get around to. Impersonality, I am convinced, can be met by reorganization of our schools and colleges into smaller units. For centuries, the great universities of Britain have consisted of small colleges, none with over 500 students. At long last, our multiversities have begun to consider the cluster college organization. The University of California at Santa Cruz, although it will ultimately have 27,500 students, will have no single college as large as 1,000 students. Two new Florida universities have adopted this cluster pattern, and at least one older Michigan university has begun to establish small colleges around individual dormitories.

But even more fundamental to personal education is the recent innovative trend to "independent study." Here is where we who work in media hold the strategic and tactical solution. More than one thoughtful educator today has agreed with Winslow Hatch, who wrote in his U.S.O.E. "New Dimension" pamphlet that the ability of a student to study independently is a measure of quality education. Individual independent study, which now dominates innovation and experimentation in more than

100 colleges and in countless schools, is completely dependent upon teacher and pupil sophistication in media use.

Imperfectly, those who experiment with independent study understand the truth that Marshall McLuhan has popularized only incidentally: the truth that for the first time in the history of education we can now match individual differences in students with individual differences in media. Our imperfections result from our inadequate knowledge of media.

This is not surprising. Our teacher education has never adequately prepared teachers to use books and libraries. In 1940, Chancellor Emeritus Harvie Branscomb authored a book called *Teaching with Books*, based on a study for the Carnegie Corporation. It angered some college faculty members because it hurt with an indisputable truth: because college faculty do not use books and libraries with sufficient sophistication, they therefore do not teach with books as they should. If this was true with the more conventional media formats of print in 1940, how much more true it is in 1969, with a range of newer formats from television to computer-assisted materials.

This inadequacy exists because teacher education, both in teacher education agencies and in liberal arts institutions, has failed to prepare teachers to teach with media. Print and non-print are considered, if at all, only in relation to a subject, to a method, or to educational psychology. Such incidental teaching of media is highly important. But it should be preceded by a *per se* introduction to media that considers the range of formats now available, and that evaluates each form for its strengths in relation to certain learning situations.

And if our teachers have had inadequate preparation in media use, think of the students they teach. At best, pupils have perhaps a dozen class periods on the use of the library, during their elementary and secondary school years. In college, they may have a perfunctory tour of the library during freshman orientation week. A few colleges offer a one-hour course in library use; even fewer make it compulsory.

Let's face it: we who work in media must take a share of the blame for the comparative neglect of media education. We have been too separated in the past. Ever since the audiovisual wave of the media movement swept into education, libraries have been stand-offish. They began calling audiovisual materials "non-book," a term which my students know has always been anathema to me. Audiovisualists, equally, began to avoid libraries, to resist any integration.

In 1935, when I introduced the first audiovisual course for librarians and teachers at Peabody College, I was considered far out in left field. After the war, when I came back to start a new school for the training of librarians at Florida State, I insisted from the start that librarians should be introduced to the whole range of media—print and non-print. In 1946, I began to bear my cross of extremists in both the audiovisual and the library camps. Some of you may recall the friendly debate I had with Ole Larson in *Education Screen*; and later with the school superintendents of San Francisco and Grosse Pointe, Michigan, in the feature forum the *NEA Journal* sponsored. In Florida, we invited the librarians and audiovisualists to meet together once a year at Florida State University. The Florida Education Association set up the first joint luncheon ever held between the two groups at a state teachers association convention. They have met every year since.

But Florida pioneered the unity concept with two exciting innovations: the first was the materials center, which combined libraries and audiovisual centers (the 1950 predecessor of what later became learning resource centers). It was inevitable that these materials centers would call for a new breed of media worker—someone with knowledge of the whole range of instructional materials found in the schools of the state. So Florida became the first state to introduce a unified certification for librarians and audiovisualists.

As more librarians and audiovisualists began to see strength in unity, and as a new generation of media workers came out of Florida State with training in both print and non-print, those who controlled the educational purse strings began to understand the role of instructional materials in learning. Our first reward was to secure special legislative funding in the form of a million dollars, earmarked for instructional materials in the schools. To equip teachers, administrators, and media workers throughout the state to work with these instructional materials, Florida State staged pre-school one-day institutes in seven geographically regional centers, for each of three successive years. Each year these institutes attracted about 1,500 educators.

I recapitulate this bit of Florida history, because in some ways you in Nebraska, with the activation of NEMA, appear to be ready to pick up the torch of unified media and carry it forward to heights we did not scale. The time is especially ripe because of the educational unrest in America, and because of our unprecedented national courage and dream for universal education. You can look at the experiences of Florida, and of other states that have had the vision—Oregon and Washington, in the West; Texas in the South; Minnesota in the Midwest; Pennsylvania in the East; and perhaps a dozen other states. You may also want to study the states where separatism has waxed fiercely; where audiovisualists and librarians have struggled with each other instead of with the obstacles to learning with media. And then go on to your program, a program that may well show the nation a new dimension in education. Before I suggest what I think this program might be, I'd like to be sure you understand what I mean by media education. Recently it has become a mark of the sophisticate to understand media the way Marshall McLuhan does. Or does he? At least one articulate professor of education, Kenneth Melvin of Boston University, a native New Zealander, doesn't think so. He writes in the *Phi Delta Kappan* (June 1967, pages 488-91), ". . . it is paucity of content no less than incoherence of form which reduces McLuhan to the ranks of the pretenders." I do not quite understand media the way McLuhan does.

Let me say, first, that I treasure the brief association I had with Professor McLuhan when I was a member of the ASCD Commission on Instructional Materials. And then let me confess to a bit of professional envy at his financial and promotional success in arousing public awareness of media as we have never been able to do in our schools and colleges. I feel, perhaps, a bit of extra covetousness because I was unable in all my writings—and especially in my book, *Instructional Materials*—to convey the basic truth about educational media, which I believe McLuhan has subordinated to spectaculars.

The basic principle about media, in my opinion, is that the format—that is, the physical makeup—of media affects communication. In education, for example, a motion picture may communicate less effectively a certain concept for an individual student at a given level of development than a transparency overlay, or a tape, or even a printed paperback. Therefore, the effective teacher must have an impartial understanding of the whole range of media formats, from textbook to television; from community resource to computer console; from graphic to projection. Thus we in education who understand media cannot permit our partiality for one format to prevent us from appreciating other formats; we cannot have mental blocks against print, or projections, or transmissions like discs and tapes, or computer-assisted materials. We respect the shutter bug; we tolerate the 16mm devotee who sometimes acts as if the motion picture, like Duz, does everything; we understand the librarian who loves to read hardcover print, and who considers everything else non-book. But we believe in media, all of them; and we believe these specialists can do less in education because of their format biases.

To the dictionary definition of media as channels of communication, I have added my definition of what I call the generic book, which includes all media formats. The generic book is the *sum total of man's communication possibilities*. As I indicated in my *Saturday Review* editorial, the generic book is man's evidence of life. You can understand, then, that in my meaning of media a film is as much a book as some communication printed on paper and bound in a hard cover. So also are maps, bulletin boards, slides, transparency overlays, models, films, microfilms, stereo discs, magnetic tapes, radio transcriptions, TV videotapes, computer learning programs, or a school journey to the salt mine.

In my book *Instructional Materials*, I classified media by format. Our courses of study, as well as certain selection aids, have grouped media by level of student development. Sometimes we group these levels K-6, 7-12, 13-14, etc. Library classification systems, like Dewey and Library of Congress, have arranged media by subject. I submit that there are three basic approaches to media selection and use—by format, by level, and by subject. And this, too, is part of understanding media, which I believe either has escaped McLuhan, or has failed to enter into his considerations.

If we accept this concept of the unity of media, we cannot help closing our ranks and uniting in the common effort to educate by matching individual differences in people with individual differences in media. We can no longer think of ourselves as librarians or audiovisualists, as information scientists, or indeed as journalists, televisionists, etc. Ours is a common mission: to communicate man's noblest deeds and deepest thoughts to the end that each generation may advance the human race.

The idea of NEMA is along the way. Together the librarians, audiovisualists, and all of the other workers in the media field can accomplish much in this restless world. We need to find a common name for our occupation. Perhaps neither "librarian" nor "audiovisualist" quite identifies us in society. Lately, some have begun to speak of us as "media specialists." I sympathize even more with those who would rather call us "media generalists." But both of these are too long and awkward. I ask you to reconsider a proposal I made some time ago—that we call ourselves "mediums."

I know the objection. Spiritualism has long used this term for an individual who claims to be a channel of communication between a spiritual and an earthly being. But physics also uses this term to mean a channel for transmission of a force or effect. I believe that we who work with media have a better claim on the word because we are human channels for transmission of communications of all kinds, between humans and their environment, between humans and humans, and who knows, some day, if parapsychology continues its present development, between earthlings and the unknown.

So I suggest for your consideration a program of action for this newly activated NEMA. It might be organized about four major objectives: 1) Certification; 2) Education; 3) Legislation; 4) Innovation. First, as a further means of unifying the media workers of Nebraska, I would suggest working with the state department of education to project certifications that would anticipate the preparation of the new breed of educational personnel that the learning revolution cries out for. To begin with, elementary and secondary teacher certification should include a basic media course to replace the present fragmentary courses in either audiovisual or library materials. The content of such a course is suggested by current requirements in some states, and by my book, *Instructional Materials*. The purpose of such a requirement is that every teacher will have the sophistication to teach with media in modernized learning resources.

Next, at the professional level for media specialists (or media generalists, or mediums), a unified certification should merge the present requirements for librarians and audiovisualists. Bases for such a merger can be found in the merged teacher education programs for educational media found at such institutions as Southern Illinois University, St. Cloud (Minnesota) State College, San Jose State University, University of Colorado, and elsewhere. Advanced certification related to the master's, sixth-year, and doctoral level of graduate education should also be planned. Nor should the growing attention to the paraprofessional—the teacher aide, the library technical assistant, and the media aide—be overlooked. Finally, media education for students in elementary and secondary schools needs a new look.

This leads to the education objective. NEMA should work hard with teacher education agencies, and especially with their departments in library science, audiovisual education, etc. If the University of Nebraska undertakes a graduate librarian program, NEMA should try to get the unity concept into their planning. With the junior colleges, paraprofessional education should be planned along the lines of the Texas Tex-Tec syllabi. Major attention should be given to teaching media use in the elementary and secondary schools, and in the colleges of Nebraska.

Legislation can be effected through the state education and library associations. Funding is, of course, at the top of the list for education media of all kinds. Also important, however, are facilities and new architectural perspective in planning educational buildings. Equipment must be modernized to capitalize on automation and computer advances.

All of this is but supportive to innovation in education, which is the only answer to campus and school unrest. Universal education with its widest range of individual differences cries out for a new learning mode. The heart of this new learning mode is independent study. To help independent study succeed, a rich range of educational media is imperative. The media center must become truly the heart of all education. Classrooms must be subordinated to learning resources; library tables must give way to carrels (preferably the wet kind, with dial access) in quantity sufficient to provide each student with his own individual workbench.

My fellow mediums of Nebraska, I salute you on the activation of NEMA. May you and your new organization show the way to your state, and to your nation, with new dimensions in education.

MEDIUM SCHOOLS AND MEDIUM TEACHERS

*A format classification of educational media reinforces the thesis
that media of innumerable physical makeups will revolutionize
library selection, teacher teaching, and student learning.*

Education is in the middle of a new revolution. One of the "never
before" causes is the objective not only of education for all, but of higher
education for everyone. This has resulted in a school population explosion.
Teacher shortages and classroom overcrowding have threatened adequacy, to
say nothing of quality. We have now in our classes the widest range of
individual differences we have ever known. Teachers are confronted with a
group teaching approach that frustrates the gifted, overwhelms the disadvantaged, and leaves the center of the "bell-shaped curve" largely unmotivated.

It is not surprising, therefore, that one of the currently developing
solutions to the problems of mass education is independent study. By their
"honors" and "autonomous" courses such colleges as Antioch in Ohio,
Presbyterian in Florida, Kendall in Illinois, Monteith in Michigan, and Santa
Cruz in California are replacing classroom teaching with library learning. By
means of the carrel, other institutions—such as Oklahoma Christian, Stephens
in Missouri, and Mount San Antonio in California—are centering instruction
at the student's private workbench, rather than in the chairs of a lecture hall.
Over 100 institutions are now experimenting with aspects of the "Library-
College," a college that is a library.

Nor is the trend toward independent study neglecting secondary or
elementary education. Notable examples can be found in the high school at
Ridgefield, Illinois; in the elementary school at Shaker Heights, Ohio; and in
the innovations wherever experimenting is part of the learning climate. There
are unmistakable signs of this revolution as the classroom becomes steadily
more dependent on the library. This dependence now takes on a new
dimension, a suggestion that the previous relationship of library to classroom
may be reversed. Instead of the library supporting the classroom, as has been
traditionally advocated by both classroom instructors and school librarians, it
may now be the library that initiates the learning, with the classroom
assuming the supporting role. Just as in higher education we see the
emergence of something now identified as the library-college,[1] so we may
also see the development, in secondary and elementary education, of
something I have called "the medium school."[2]

THE MEDIUM SCHOOL

The medium school may be defined as the school in which independent
study with individually tailored educational media is the basic learning mode.
Class or group meetings and discussions become activities to fill student-
initiated needs for supplementary information, or perspective, not available in
the media collection. The medium school aims to match individual

Reprinted with permission from *APLA Bulletin*, 33:6-13 (December 1969).

differences in pupils with individual differences in media, thereby realizing more adequately than ever before the individualized nature of learning.

What makes possible the medium school concept, for the first time, is the quantity and the range of media now available. What prevents realization of the ultimate medium school are the habits of learning engendered by the classroom-lockstep, group approach. What handicaps full utilization of the medium school concept is the inadequate preparation of our teacher personnel to perform in this learning posture. This applies not only to the classroom instructor, but also to those presently designated as librarians or audiovisualists.

The medium school is not without antecedent. Right after World War II the "materials center" movement began, probably in Florida, and possibly as a result of the idea for a new, accredited, graduate library school at Florida State University. Fundamental to the educational objective of this new school was the aim of educating a new generation of librarians who would be aware of the whole range of instructional materials used in our schools. It was proposed that library school students study not only such ideas as come in print of every form (such as books, magazines, newspapers, documents, or manuscripts), but also the ideas that come through pictures and motion pictures, on discs and tapes, over radio and TV, through community resources, and, more lately, through so-called programmed print, teaching machines, and computer consoles.

Hence was born, in Florida, the materials center. Once and for all, the librarian term "non-book materials" became anathema. Instead, the idea of the "generic book" came about.[3] Regardless of the format, any record or communication by man is a book. Out of this came the Florida idea of an "instructional materials specialist." Florida was the first state in the union to offer a single school certification in instructional materials that brought together personnel heretofore separately designated in some state school systems as either librarians or audiovisualists. Sometimes referred to as a "shotgun marriage," this unity concept has proven sound, and has been adopted by at least a dozen states.

THE MEDIA

Fundamental to the success of the medium school is the concept of media. An educational medium can be defined as any means of communication between teachers and pupils. Media may be classified in at least three basic ways: a) by format; b) by level; and c) by subject. Our most common subject classification of materials is the Dewey Decimal System, used by over 95 percent of our school libraries. The accepted level arrangement of media is by the grade groupings of K-6 and 7-12. Sometimes, as in the *Children's Catalog*,[4] materials are arranged grade by grade.

Format classification of materials was incorporated in my book *Instructional Materials*. The term "format" as used by librarians means the physical make-up of a medium. By last count, over 100 physical forms of materials have been identified in our nation's schools. In the figure on the next page, I have attempted to classify educational media by format.

Print continues to be the most important class of education media, not

EDUCATIONAL MEDIA: A FORMAT CLASSIFICATION

Class	Group	Examples
I. PRINT	1. Textbook	Workbook, manual
	2. Reference book	Dictionary, encyclopedia
	3. Reading book	Fiction, poetry
	4. Serial	Periodical, newspaper
II. GRAPHIC	5. Map	Globe, chart
	6. Picture	Photo, drawing
	7. Exhibit	Bulletin board, diorama
	8. Object	Specimen, model
III. PROJECTION	9. Opaque (still)	Picture, object
	10. Transparent (still)	Overlay, slide
	11. Motion picture	Time-lapse, 3-D
	12. Miniature	Microbioscope, microfilm
IV. TRANSMISSION	13. Disc	Monaural, stereo
	14. Tape	Cartridge, reel
	15. Radio	FM, transcription
	16. Television	Closed circuit, videotape
V. PROGRAMMED	17. Print	Programmed text
	18. Machine	Teaching machine
	19. Community resource	Natural, human
	20. Computer	Console, dial access

only quantitatively, but qualitatively as well. For a long time to come, heavy reliance on the product of the printing press must continue. Its format still offers, through its quantitative head start and through its primary nature as a medium, the best individual approach to learning. In the one-to-one ratio of medium to learner, the print formats are probably as economical in time and money as any.

Although the textbook went through a cycle of disparagement, its position has been restored. It still provides the gateway to media learning. By its survey, organization, and bibliography it sets the stage for the media to follow.

In the parade of educational media, there is no division of print that is less effectively used by teacher and student than the reference book. Except for the dictionary, encyclopedia, and perhaps atlas groups, the thousand or so titles on the open shelves of the main reading room in college and school libraries never enter the mainstream of the learning process. This was painfully illustrated the other day when a distinguished physicist discovered the 105th annual issue of the *Statesman's Year Book* on my desk while our conversation was suspended by a telephone call. "Where has this book been all of my academic life?" Unashamedly he admitted he had never heard of the book before. As a librarian I feel no exaltation over this; only a deep sense of failure about the impotence of our teaching of library use.

My own lifelong interest in the literature of reference was probably awakened by an accident. During my high school senior year I elected an introductory course in economics. The fact that the instructor happened to be the lady teacher who had first aroused my deepest feelings of romance only reinforced my interest in this curriculum subject. Accordingly, I decided to read the article on economics in the *Britannica*, first, and then in two other encyclopedias. Armed with this overview of the semester's commitment, I anticipated each unit as it was introduced by the teacher and the text. When the course developed as the encyclopedias had indicated, I triumphed inwardly, and often outwardly, in recitations and in themes of increased understanding. When the presentation by teacher or textbook took a different route, I objected, either to myself or, on occasion, with a demonstrative recitation or essay. This encyclopedia overview device helped me to an "A" in that course, and in many subsequent college courses, where I always anticipated my subjects for the term with a pre-semester encyclopedia overview.

Among the graphics, maps and globes were always my favorites. I discovered early what an analemma is, and I was captivated later by the whole idea of calendar and time in relation to the sun. When during my Fulbright year in the United Kingdom I accomplished the travel objective of visiting Greenwich, just outside London, and standing on zero longitude, I had been fully prepared by my study of place media. Incidentally, are maps and globes audiovisual, or library media? You know that there is always a whole chapter on maps and globes in such standard audiovisual texts as Wittich and Schuller.[5] There is also a chapter on maps and globes in my reference textbook for librarians. Some school systems I know keep maps and globes in the school library, but charge their purchase to the audiovisual budget. Wouldn't it be silly to ask the child, "What kind of globe did you consult, a library globe, or an audiovisual globe?"

The same is true of pictures. No one knows how many years librarians have maintained picture files. But we do know that in audiovisual instruction we have something we call "flat" pictures. The term, of course, has nothing to do with the subject; it refers to the lack of a third dimension. Incidentally, 3-D pictures appeared in our libraries, as well as our living rooms, in the form of stereopticon projectors, many years before the AV movement was born.

When it comes to transmissions, a few of us will remember back to about 1928 when the Carnegie Corporation gave college libraries a million dollars with which to purchase phonograph records. These are discs in our AV terminology, and they are still a very important format among educational media. Our materials centers in Florida set up in the reading rooms something we called "Listening Posts." A record player, a jack, and as many as eight sets of earphones put us into the cross-media business. Youngsters could sit at the reading room table, read *Hamlet,* and listen to John Gielgud do it out loud through their earphones. The procedure disturbed no one else in the reading room. We do this better now in our "wet carrels," by remote dialing.

Since 1947 we have reinforced the disc format with the tape, gaining even finer fidelity than is available in the hi-fi disc or in stereo. The tape can accomplish what no other format in our whole repertoire of media can even imitate. For example, one of the most touching foreign language teaching devices I know is our Florida tape exchanges with schools in Colombia and other Latin American nations. A teacher can talk her heart out in an effort to induce pupils to imitate the precise accent. But how much more readily will our high school youngsters listen for nuances in the taped voices of Latin American teenagers who talk about subjects of adolescent interest.

Some of my colleagues accuse me of favoring the transparency overlay above all other media formats. Indeed, my teachers know I am leaving for an off-campus extension course by the fact that I am carrying the comparatively lightweight, overhead projector out to my car. With the transparency, I can teach concepts of reference like the cumulative feature of the Wilson indexes, or the unique three-column arrangement of Ames's *Comprehensive Index* to U.S. government publications probably more enlighteningly than through any other medium format. I believe so much in the transparency that the encyclopedia of which I am editor-in-chief was one of the first to introduce the transparency overlay into its pages.[6] Sometimes as I display our overlay on the anatomy of the frog to an audiovisual group, I half expect, by the looks on some of their faces, to be sued for crossing a printed book with something they consider exclusively audiovisual.

When most people think audiovisual, they probably think 16mm motion picture. But I am afraid the anti-audiovisual librarian thinks not medium, but the mechanics of the projector through which the film must be shown. If you look at the motion picture as just another format of the generic book, then you consider film the way a medium teacher, or a medium librarian does. How does this format contribute more effectively to a learning experience than any other format in my whole repertoire of communication? I have my answer. Indeed, I have several answers.

Let me illustrate with two. For years I used to take my students to a paper mill to see (and smell) how paper is made. This subject is important to librarians. And I consider the field trip another medium for communicating community resources. But even this format has limitations. Several times I observed elementary classes on school journeys there. The more aggressive children, not over six out of thirty, would get close up to the process; the rest would strain for a view, and after a while retire away from the scene of action and become involved in unrelated activities. I had somewhat the same problem with my college students. Then I discovered two 16mm motion pictures that followed the process closely for all of my students in a way that even the most ideal conditions on a field trip rarely approached. The film was the best format for the purpose of that learning situation, in my opinion.

Then there was the botany professor whose home was across the street from ours. I knew him well enough to know that he was unaware of the new phenomenon known as time-lapse photography. I wondered how he could teach about flowers very excitingly without the wonder of petals unfolding instantly before your very eyes through time-lapse. There was only one way to handle this without hurting him and bringing him down on the library and the librarian forever.

"Max," I said one day in our living room, "will you help me out? I've been asked to review a new film in botany. You know how little I know about this subject. Would you review it for me?" Max agreed to help me out, as a neighbor, and friend, and above all, an authority advising a layman. What happened was what I had hoped.

"It's fantastic. How long has this technique been available?" He had forgotten about what I had asked him to do for me. From that time on he was an avid user of time-lapse photography, and a much better teacher for his students.

Perhaps I have illustrated what I call the power of media formats in communication and teaching. My point is that we must, as teachers and librarians, know the whole range of instructional materials, and use them without favoritism or prejudice, depending upon the learning situation at hand. And I contend that none of us can do that if, as librarians, we refer to some media as "non-book materials"; or if, as audiovisualists, we generously concede that books will not be entirely replaced by audiovisual materials. There is no Berlin wall between us. We are all in this media business together. There is a high mission for us: to communicate educationally as education never has communicated before. We have within our concept the means to make universal education possible for the first time in history. Now at long last we can match individual differences in students with individual differences in materials. Not since Binet, Cattell, and others made education aware of the truth of individual differences have the schools and colleges been able to do anything about it. Now we who work with media can show the way, if librarians and audiovisualists will unite their efforts instead of condescending toward each other. That union can be effected in the library.

THE LEARNING RESOURCE CENTER

Call the library anything you want. I am sympathetic to any variation on this name that will draw us together. We in Florida introduced the term materials center. This was soon modified to materials resource center, to instructional materials center, and then to learning resources center. You will undoubtedly find many other variations on this name. Some of you may not like this, but basically all of these are a true library. Because I mean something different by the word library than does the traditional librarian. I claim to have introduced one of the first—if not the very first—audiovisual courses in the South at Peabody as early as 1935. Evidence is in print. And Florida State was the first accredited graduate school in librarianship to require all librarians in training to be audiovisually educated.

At Florida State Library School we started the present education media center which serves the university and the state. We merged all formats in our catalog, and our librarian published the first manual on integrated cataloging, about 1948.

You can see that I am a rabid audiovisualist. I believe the movement did much for librarianship, as well as for education in general. It not only broadened the librarian's concept of the generic book, but it also taught librarianship how to become less passive and more dynamic in the education role—just as another periphery, information science, is now showing traditional reference how to use the computer and take an initiatory part in research.

For nearly two decades I bore the cross of bringing us together. I was crucified by both librarians and audiovisualists at their respective meetings. Although we succeeded in developing a uniform certification, we could never agree on a professional designation. Audiovisualists didn't want to be called librarians; librarians didn't want to be called audiovisualists. Eventually, at FSU, we became "instructional materials specialists." Over the years a new generation has come into being in Florida: media specialists who truly disregard the artificial boundary line between AV and library. They are the leaders in our materials center movement.

A materials center can be defined as a library, or learning resource center, which acquires, organizes and disseminates all media formats, subjects, and levels pertinent to its educational objective. To accomplish this, media are selected by the community served to further communication between teacher and pupil. After acquisition, these media are cataloged and indexed in one sequence, so that a subject approach to the catalog will reveal not only books and other print available, but pictures, transparencies, slides, filmstrips, motion pictures, discs, tapes, radio and TV programs, community resources, programmed and computer-assisted instructional materials.

In the dissemination of these media, the library, or materials center, or learning resource center, has an educational role of its own. It recognizes the validity of Winslow Hatch's measure of quality education as including the degree to which a student can study independently.[7] And therefore the newer library is increasingly geared to the idea that relations between classroom and library may be reversed. The librarian or media specialist who is not frittering his effort away in an internecine war is harnessing the unified resources of the library to give meaning to the relentless independent study trend in all of our education.

He is doing this, with respect to facilities, by revising upward all of the previous library and audiovisual standards. No longer are we proud to claim that we can seat 25 percent of our student body at one time. Nothing less than 100 percent will satisfy us. Indeed, Oklahoma Christian College provides for growth by including seating for 110 percent.[8] Nor is the library resource center satisfied with the old-fashioned reading room table. The Ford Foundation has produced a booklet[9] which shows 16 variations on designs for the individual carrel. Among these designs is a plan for converting tables, economically, without the loss of reader accommodation. Indicated also are provisions for increasingly "wet" carrels. (A wet carrel can be identified as one that provides dial, or remote, access to a variety of media formats in a library.)

The carrel is basic to the materials center concept of education. If independent study is to mean anything, every student must have his own individual workbench where he can report for hard work, where he can begin to learn the facts of life, under conditions he must face when he begins to earn a living. By means of this facility the library resource center further emphasizes the unity of media. Above all, through the carrel, the library reinforces individual independent study as the fundamental learning mode.

THE NEW BREED FACULTY

Some insecurity accompanies all innovation. The trend to independent study should encourage and stimulate all faculty who love to teach—faculty in classrooms, and faculty in libraries—because under the independent study revolution the line between librarians and classroom instructors will become as indistinct as the artificial boundary between audiovisual and other media.

In this kind of education, the teacher becomes fundamentally a media counsellor and an inspirer. He selects and prescribes media for the individual much as the doctor prescribes for the patient. The student goes to his carrel, reads, views, hears, and even smells, tastes and touches. He goes on field trips into the community. There is a new kind of laboratory, the audiotutorial type pioneered at Purdue, that can occur at the student's workbench. The student writes, as well as reads; he speaks, performs, manipulates. There are class meetings, and smaller group discussions, but they grow out of student need for resolving of conflicts, for amplifications, for points of view. And there are lectures by a faculty member that cover ground or perspective different from what is available in the ready-made media.

Obviously, such a new breed of faculty needs to know media as our faculty today generally do not; as even our librarians and audiovisualists don't. They need to go through a teacher education that is different from what we know. Primarily, they need a teacher education that will stop teaching media *incidentally*—incidental to subject, method, psychology, or what not. Somewhere in teacher education, media need to be taught *per se*. And they need to be taught in the proper perspective.

Today, if teacher education teaches media *per se* at all, it does so along three different avenues that are frequently independent of each other. One of these avenues is the English course in children's literature. Another avenue is the library science course on library use. The third avenue is the course or courses for teachers in audiovisual education. These separate courses are almost as injurious to the cause of independent study education as no *per se* attention at all to media. Because in each case there is a distorted emphasis on one format or another—hardcover, film, tape, computer, or TV.

What is needed is an articulated program of media education in our teacher training. Articulation does not mean a program in library science with a course that gives some attention to so-called "non-book" materials. Nor does it mean an audiovisual program of courses that is allergic to print, on the flimsy excuse that everyone already reads books. The same could be said for TV; for indeed, who today does not watch TV some of the time? Neither does the audiovisual department educate teachers properly by setting up two programs, one exclusively allergic to reading material, the other integrating library science with audiovisual courses.

The road to adequate media education for teachers and librarians is now being opened up at such places as Southern Illinois University,[10] San Jose State, Purdue, and elsewhere. In these programs the first course is an introduction to media, such as is comprehended by my book *Instructional Materials*. Successive courses, for media specialists, are a balanced merging of the AACTE undergraduate program for librarians and the DAVI recommendations for audiovisualists.

The next generation of librarians and audiovisualists, and of media-minded teachers and administrators, has the future of education in its hands. I believe the media schools and the library-colleges now in the making will be the means by which the United States of America will achieve universal education, for the first time in the history of the world.

FOOTNOTES

1. Louis Shores, *The Library-College* (Philadelphia, Drexel, 1966).

2. Shores, "The Medium School," *Phi Delta Kappan*, February, 1966.

3. Shores, *Instructional Materials* (New York, Ronald Press, 1960), Chapter I.

4. *Children's Catalog* (Bronx, N.Y., H. W. Wilson, 1941), pp. 1069ff. (This feature is no longer continued, however.)

5. Walter A. Wittich and Charles F. Schuller, *Audio-Visual Materials: Their Nature and Use*, 4th ed., Harper's Exploration Series in Education (New York, Harper & Row, 1967).

6. *Collier's Encyclopedia* (1970), Vol. 10, p. 422, and transparency overlay following, "Anatomy of the Frog."

7. Winslow Hatch, *New Dimensions in Higher Education* (Washington, U.S. Office of Education, 1966).

8. Oklahoma Christian College, *The Sound of Learning* (Oklahoma City, 1966), tape, notebook.

9. John Beynon, *Study Carrels: Designs for Independent Study Space* (Stanford, Calif., Ford Foundation Educational Facilities Laboratory, 1964), 20p.

10. Southern Illinois University, *Report on Library-Audiovisual Instruction* (Carbondale, 1966), Chapter 23.

PART II:

THE MATERIALS CENTER

ENTER THE MATERIALS CENTER

The concept of the materials center, forerunner of the learning resource center, first entered educational and library thinking in Florida in about 1947, spearheaded by the Florida State University School of Library Science. By 1955, distinctions between the materials center and the school library could be identified as they are here.

Librarians not in the school field have recently begun to hear that the historic term "library" is about to give way to another agency in our elementary and secondary education. To some academic and public librarians the appearance of the "materials center" is added evidence that school librarians are a different species, perhaps only distantly related to the profession of which they are a recognized division. But to a great many other librarians the metamorphosis of the school library, occurring contemporaneously with other startling educational developments, suggests the possibility of counterparts in the community and on the campus.

What is this new agency, the materials center? As yet, the literatures of both education and librarianship are exceedingly unrevealing. The sparsity of writings can be attributed in part to the recency of the subject. But to an even greater extent much of the hesitancy about written expression is due to uncertainty over the real nature of the materials center movement.

As a starting definition, the materials center is the agency in our American schools responsible for the acquisition, organization and dissemination of all instructional materials used in the learning process. This says at once that the materials center performs its role "not by books alone" but by every medium useful to teacher and pupil in furthering education. The range of materials, encompassing all those we now call "audiovisual," is one of the basic differences between a materials center and a school library.

But that is not the only difference. The relative position of the various kinds of instructional materials also distinguishes the materials center. For example, in considerable library literature, reference to "non-book" materials is still accepted terminology. Likewise in audiovisual writings, such as the very fine brochure number 3 of the Department of Audio-Visual Instruction, the impression is left that print or so-called "verbal" materials are an appendage. Neither one of these approaches quite describes the concept of the content of a true materials center.

A preliminary inventory of school materials in Florida, for example, reveals some two score classes of media used by teachers and pupils in the learning process. Without identifying all of them here, it is possible through partial enumeration to indicate something of the potential range of content in the materials center of tomorrow.

To begin with, the textbook is a fundamental instructional medium. With its supplementary workbooks, study guides, and assorted teaching aids, it constitutes an important class of materials center accessions. Despite acquisition, organization, and circulation procedures greatly different from

Reprinted with permission from *ALA Bulletin*, 49:285-88 (June 1955).

those followed for conventional library materials, textbooks must be considered an integral part of the materials center content.

It goes without saying that the traditional core of a school library—books and magazines—also constitutes a major element of the materials center collection, as do pamphlets, newspapers, clippings, pictures, charts, and other items librarians have long considered essentials of their vertical file. Bulletin boards have always accented the library's exhibit and display services. And from time to time various collections of art and science objects have been absorbed in the school library collection. Maps and globes have certainly been almost standard library equipment. But it is interesting to note that recently some school libraries have begun to charge these to their "audiovisual budget."

Which brings us to the third great division of the materials center collection. The previous paragraph mentions no fewer than six classes of instructional materials that are claimed as stock in trade by both school librarians and audiovisualists. This underlines the thin gray line between audiovisual and non-audiovisual materials, which may or may not exist, depending on how much of a separatist the school librarian or the audiovisualist may be.

To the separatist in the two conventional camps the 16mm motion picture is the audiovisual symbol. Almost as symbolic is the filmstrip. Other audiovisual media, probably in descending degrees of anti-verbalism and anti-abstraction are disc and tape recordings, radio, television, and the field trip.

These are by no means all of the 40 classes of instructional materials used in our schools, but they give an idea of the expanded scope of the materials center collection. In addition, they emphasize the content difference between a school library and a materials center. In the former, "books and other materials" is still the vogue; in the latter, all are instructional materials, and each class of media has its particular contribution to make to an individual learning situation in which teacher and pupil create conditions as individual as fingerprints.

Which brings us to a second important difference between the materials center and the school library. Although historically the school library can be said to have begun as a way of learning, in the years of struggle for funds and recognition, the educational ends have often been subordinated to the means. It is an irrefutable tenet that better learning occurs in an orderly house. The devotion to organization of the school library by generations of school librarians has been no inconsiderable contribution. Inevitably, however, such consecration has sometimes resulted in second things coming first.

This point is illustrated by two quotes that represent the difference between the school library concept, on the one hand, and the emerging materials center idea. One common quotation is this: "I am so overworked now with just books and magazines that I cannot take on the additional responsibilities of audiovisual." This is a school library point of view. The materials center point of view does not see that choice. To one who works in a materials center, the either-or might just as logically be, "I am so overworked now with books that I haven't time for magazines." Or, to put it another way, and more positively, the materials center person believes that all classes of instructional materials are his responsibility in the proportions required by the school program. Fundamentally, he does not believe his profession is a mission of formats as much as it is of ideas. The materials center has as its high aim the dissemination of good ideas in the form best understood by the individual child.

The other quote which distinguishes the school librarian's thinking from that of the materials center person is this one: "I am so far behind in my cataloging that I shall have to neglect nearly everything else until I am caught up." Now, the materials center person has a high regard for the accessibility that comes from good organization. But the materials center librarian is thinking these days most enthusiastically about cooperative cataloging, acquisition, and other organizational activities.

Which brings us to a third difference. The materials center tends toward greater dispersion than is found in the school library. As viewed today there are three echelons of materials centers service. The top echelon is the center-city or county-school system. This is the control for all of the centers. It performs the organizational tasks—acquisitions, classification, cataloging, and other technical processes for all of the centers in the system. In this system center is the vast reservoir of materials on which any of the subordinate centers can call to supplement its own resources. In the system center is the central inventory, a kind of union catalog for all varieties of materials found anywhere in the school system.

The next echelon consists of the school materials centers. This middle echelon is the control for all the centers in classrooms in the building, as well as in other places. It houses, in quarters differently planned from the quarters previously recommended for school libraries, the whole range of instructional materials required by the school it serves. Its materials come from the system center fully classified, cataloged, and largely processed for immediate use. The school center's concern is largely with the problem of dissemination to the classrooms and other points of learning.

The third echelon is the classroom. It too is a materials center. For the classroom today has almost no resemblance to that of yesterday. Such a "3-D" classroom, as heralded in the NEA exhibit of a few months back, is a tribute to the multi-materials concept of teaching and learning. Indeed, such a classroom is a tangible acknowledgement of the educational theory that inspired the leaders of both the school library and the audiovisual movements before the techniques of book charging and film booking became major professional absorptions.

The first part of this century produced the distinguished psychologist J. McKeen Cattell, father of "individual differences." The psychological principle was made to order for librarianship, since it proved that no two individuals in the world brought exactly the same preparation to a learning situation. Thus, since even the best group teaching methods would not meet the needs of the individual learner, what was needed was a method or a device so flexible that learning could be custom tailored to the unique figure that distinguishes each human.

Such American educators as Horace Mann, W. T. Harris, and William Russell, among others, saw immediately the method in the multi-materials concept and the device in the increasing quantity and variety of instructional media. From these educators and others like them came the first impetus to the earlier school library movement and the later audiovisual operation. From librarians who sensed the power of their calling and from audiovisualists who later shared this concept came the embryo of the present materials center idea.

At the moment the school librarians are doing the most with this teaching aspect of librarianship. They are in the vanguard of a movement within our profession to recall us to our educational responsibility. In the history of American library service, academic, public, and special librarians have each, as groups, made significant contributions to the body of professional principle and practice shared by all librarianship. And now it appears that school librarians are about to make one of the most significant of all contributions to our profession with the materials center. By means of this multi-material concept alone, librarianship may provide the key to mass education. Led by the school librarians on the elementary and secondary levels, and followed by the academic librarians on the college level and the public librarians on the adult level, librarianship may yet assume its rightful educational role and provide the answer to the doubts about the possibility of universal education. Looked at in that way, the materials center does not replace but rather augments the mission of the library.

PORTRAIT OF A MATERIALS CENTER

This 1955 article is the embryo of the 1969 AASL-DAVI Standards. Although the ALA Bulletin *had already arranged with the* Peabody Journal of Education *to include this in its school library issue, the decision was subsequently overruled, probably because the concept was too far ahead of its time. I could not but agree considering the strong opposition from separatist audio-visualists and separatist librarians even in our pioneering state of Florida. The crusade for the unity concept was a long and hard struggle.*

Everywhere in our American schools today we hear the term "materials center." It is a term that is rapidly replacing such terms as school library and audiovisual center. To many, the materials center is merely the union of the library and the audiovisual center; actually, the materials center is much more than that. Essentially, it is the culmination of an educational concept—a concept so basic that it may well save the day for America's courageous attempt to accomplish what no other nation in the world's history has undertaken before: complete and continuing education for all of the people from cradle to grave.

In one word, this concept may be called multi-materials. In a few more words it may be simply stated that good teaching is good communication between teacher and pupil; and the key to good communication is acquaintance with and accessibility to a wide range of instructional materials. Providing such acquaintance and accessibility for teachers and pupils is the mission of the materials center.

How the materials center does this today varies from separate and conventional school libraries or audiovisual centers, in some schools, to integrated resource centers in entire school systems. Between these two extremes are various degrees of evolution toward the ultimate materials center. What that ultimate materials center will be is still open to experiment and discussion. What it will probably not be seems more certain.

It does not appear likely that the American school will "go for" separate audiovisual and library centers in each building. Economically, the small school cannot afford such separation, and most American schools are still small. Educationally, it is almost impossible to divide instructional materials into "audiovisual" and "non-audiovisual." Even if one accepts symbolically the 16mm motion picture as "audiovisual," and the book as symbolically "library," there are still some two score additional classes of materials that are claimed by both librarians and audiovisualists. For example, the audiovisualist speaks of "flat pictures" and the librarian of "picture files," yet both terms describe approximately the same instructional materials. There is a considerable audiovisual professional literature about "recordings" and an equally voluminous library professional literature about "records." Nor should the teacher be expected to ask the child whether he has an audiovisual globe or a library globe when they are one and the same globe.

Reprinted with permission from the *Peabody Journal of Education*, 33:66-74 (September 1955).

Basically the school library movement and the audiovisual movement are successive waves of the same educational concept: individual differences in children can best be met by individually tailored communications media.

THE MATERIALS CENTER TEACHER

We begin our portrait of a materials center with a soul. Directing this operation in the school is a good teacher—one so good that he could return to the classroom and demonstrate not only good teaching, but exciting new ways to arouse, stimulate, and inspire children. Call him librarian, audiovisualist, building coordinator of materials, materials specialist, or materials teacher. The label is of secondary importance. The important thing is that the job is assigned to a superior teacher, teacher-educated and certificated, who has seen the vision of multi-materials and who can lead the school in developing a real multi-materials education.

Then give this teacher the specialized education in instructional materials he will need. Let him have this specialty on a teacher education base, preferably on the graduate level, but acceptably, too, on the undergraduate level as part of his specialization area. His knowledge of all kinds of materials should be as thorough as his knowledge of children from his educational psychology, and of teaching method from his education courses. He should learn the content of children's and young people's books, magazines, films, filmstrips, tape and disc recordings, graphics, radio, television, and some two score other categories of school materials including the local resources for field journeys. He should gain skill in the operation of projectors and playbacks and other necessary equipment. He should learn sources for acquiring these media, criteria for evaluation and selection, techniques for classifying and cataloging, charging and booking, and above all the ways and means of utilizing these materials in the interest of better learning.

THE MATERIALS CENTER SUITE

Now let us proceed from the teacher to the question of housing. Give the materials center generous space, much more generous space than is accorded it in most schools. And let it not be an afterthought. No architect has a right to put "school" in front of his specialty who has ever been party to designing a building without provision for library or materials center. Nor can an administrator who has shared in such an omission ever be considered an educator. The full materials center is a suite of rooms encompassing at least seven distinct functions.

One of these functions is activity. This requires a room by itself, because here both the "pin-drop principal" and the "tip-toe librarian" will be unhappy. But the materials specialist, the materials teacher, and above all the pupil, will be exceedingly happy, because here a very important part of the multi-materials way of learning will be carried on.

Let me describe the activity room in the materials center suite as I see it in my mind's eye. It will be very *unlike* a library reading room. It will be very *like* a supermarket. Instead of upright shelves with books arranged six feet, ten inches high, there will be many counters and tables. Each counter or table, instead of featuring a particular kind of vegetable or meat or staple grocery, will feature a teaching unit. Over here will be a table entirely devoted to a fourth-grade weather unit; over there another table devoted to a third-grade North American Indian unit; and on a third counter an entire unit on the home. Each of the other tables and counters will feature a unit currently the concern of one classroom learning situation.

On each of these unit tables will be a selection of every type of instructional material: books, magazines, pamphlets, and documents, of course. But also recordings, tapes, filmstrips, slides, films, posters, pictures, cartoons, realia, stereographs, puppets, and, to avoid further listings of categories, *et cetera*. There will also be "target folders," a term that describes a medium that Air Force Intelligence devised for its pilots who were about to visit enemy territory for the purpose of bombing objectives. These target folders describe, by word and picture, all of the local resources of the area to be visited—both natural and artificial resources. Although these folders were devised in time of war with a destructive purpose, they suggest a most constructive idea in time of peace for our schools.

The target folder in the school materials center can do much to make the field journey a meaningful teaching medium. Each target folder should describe a local resource so as to be helpful to the teacher and class about to embark on a field trip. There will be a target folder for the local water works, airport, paper mill, phosphate mine, shoe factory, department store, newspaper, or whatever else has a potential contribution to learning. In this folder will be the name of the person to contact, the route or transportation to and from, the diary of the last class visit, with suggestions and cautions for improving the next trip, and such pictures, diagrams, questions, regulations, and other information as will be helpful.

There will also be a "Listening Post" on each or every other table to that recordings may be heard through several sets of earphones without disturbance. And there will be convenient viewers for slides and stereos.

The activity room, however, is primarily an exploration room rather than a reading, or viewing, or studying room. Here a very important part of the multi-material way of learning is carried on. Together teacher and pupil come to the materials center to shop for teaching and learning materials. As they enter the door they pick up a basket on wheels just as they would in a supermarket. They proceed to their unit table and begin to examine and rummage among the varieties of materials. Each pupil attempts to discover, evaluate, and select for himself materials that arouse his individual background. It may be that a picture or a slide or a book or a magazine article tells him best what he wants to know about the unit they are studying. Then he puts it in his basket with the intention of studying, exhibiting, expounding, and defending its content and form to his classmates. At the end of the hour, pupils and teacher will have gathered together in their baskets enough different materials to create a classroom materials center on their unit that will provide real learning opportunities for the period of time agreed on.

This then is the activity room. It serves pupil and teacher in the important exploratory stage of learning. Essentially, it provides a learning situation as important as any the teacher and child can create in their home room. The activity room alone gives the lie to the artificial distinction some school systems make between so-called "teaching" and "non-teaching" personnel. Because in the activity room, as elsewhere in the materials center, classroom teacher and materials center teacher are teaching together as creatively and industriously as anywhere in the school. And it is quite evident that pupil activity in a classroom becomes good as it approaches the quality of pupil activity in the materials center.

A second distinct function of the materials center is orientation. Here pupils learn the skills essential to efficient materials use. The tachyscope, ophthalmograph, and other reading devices provide analysis and practice opportunities for pupil and teacher. Projectors of all kinds—motion picture, slide, opaque—are available for instruction in equipment use and for viewing projected materials selected in the activity room. Playbacks and recorders for tape and disc, graphics tables, and equipment and supplies for creating school-made materials present additional learning opportunities.

A third function is study, and a properly insulated and isolated study room needs to be provided. Let it never be forgotten that much learning still goes on without physical movement. Some place in the materials center suite there is need for a quiet, study and reading room. Here a little corner for the teacher and her professional collection might well be preserved.

A fourth function, conference and group discussion, requires a place where students and teachers can meet and confer and talk. The conference room need not be large.

The other three functions of the materials center are largely organizational and administrative, since a good materials center must be well organized for use.

The first of these functions is storage. A stack room (which might be better understood if it were called a stock room) shelves, as economically as possible, the collection of materials. This stock room should have a variety of shelving, cabinets, files, and other receptacles to accommodate books, magazines, newspapers, films, filmstrips, recordings, tapes, slides, and again the *et cetera*. This is the part of the materials center that would most resemble the conventional library and audiovisual centers. From this organized stock would be taken the selections for the unit counters in the activity room.

The next of these organizational functions is booking and charging, which would take place at the control desk, the point of reception and disbursement for all materials. Here pupils and teachers would come with baskets of materials to be charged and returned. Here also could come pupils and teachers from the study and orientation rooms to charge books and to book films. It is a function that should be performed almost wholly by pupil assistants or by clerical workers. The professional library, materials teacher, or coordinator should never be burdened with these routines to the detriment of the teaching function. In this charging and booking area will be the card catalog and the various periodical indexes, also.

The final organizational function is technical processes. These usually are accomplished in a workroom, which must have running water in it. Here many of the behind-the-scenes routines are performed. It is hoped that no classification and cataloging will be necessary at the school level, since the trend is for this job to be done in the school system materials center for all schools. It is hoped, too, that less and less of the processing that has tied down so much of the school librarian's time will be done at the building level. Nevertheless, some processing will have to be done, and here again it is hoped that help in the form of pupil assistants or clerical workers will relieve the professional teacher or librarian or coordinator.

These then are the seven functions and the seven units of a school materials center at the building level, which represents the middle echelon in a materials center system. Each of these middle echelons is a key link between the overall materials center in the county or city headquarters of the school system and the classroom materials centers in the building. Recognition of these other two echelons of materials centers service completes the concept of the new school materials program.

THE CLASSROOM CENTER

Essentially, the so-called "3-D Classroom" exhibited recently by the NEA is a materials center. It is designed and equipped to utilize every one of the two score classes of school materials: it can be darkened for projection; it is wired for sound; it comes equipped with TV and radio. It is in all essence a small materials center, helping to prove that there are no essential differences between the so-called classroom teacher and the materials center teacher, librarian, or audiovisualist. Look at a good socialized recitation or at any other group activity in a classroom and you are immediately struck with its comparability to a materials center.

The classroom center should be equipped physically and pedagogically to receive materials from the building materials center. These materials should be selected periodically by teachers and pupils from their shopping trips as needed for the current unit. Materials and equipment should not remain permanently in the classroom but should be changed to meet the needs of the unit under study. The classroom that has had the same pictures on the wall and the same books on the shelves for as long as the teacher has occupied that room is losing an environmental advantage for learning. The change of pace occasioned by frequent swapping of materials through the building center is an unquestioned means of classroom stimulation.

THE SYSTEM CENTER

The system center in the county or city headquarters has a quite different function from either the building or the classroom center. The system center is the wholesaler, just as the building center is the retailer, and the classroom center the ultimate consumer. To the system center come classroom teacher and materials center teacher together to find supplements for particular units on which the building center needs help. In the system center all teachers find professional help in a good pedagogical library and in curriculum guides. The system center classifies and catalogs all materials for all schools, and maintains a central system inventory so that materials may be located in any school in the system. The system center buys for all schools, thus gaining the benefit of the better discounts. It offers a cooperative reference service to all teachers and in general performs many of the inter-library functions that are part of good regional cooperation on a research level.

This then is the concept of the materials center for our schools. It has not yet fully arrived. But here and there, in Florida and Texas, in Oregon and New York, in countless counties and cities, the new concept is tangibly revealing itself through numerous signs. Steadily we see separate audiovisual and library centers in some schools merging into integrated materials centers. Increasingly we hear of librarians and audiovisualists becoming directors and supervisors of instructional materials. Certification trends point to the recognition of a cross between the librarian and audiovisualist in the person of a materials teacher. And this is all to the good for better learning and teaching.

For the school administrator, today, there is no one development that offers more educational promise than the materials center. To take advantage of its full potential, the school principal must first understand that audiovisual and library are two aspects of a school materials program that must be planned, organized, and administered together. Second, he must secure the services of a teacher with broad training in the whole range of materials—audiovisual as well as print. Third, he must provide adequate housing for this important function of materials service. Finally, adequate financing is an inevitable requirement.

From this investment of thought, personnel, space, and funds, the return to good teaching and learning is limitless.

SYSTEM 68

My 1962 design for library-centered schools was not quite what education and school librarian were ready to accept, since I was anticipating the trend to independent study for secondary and elementary education, as well as for undergraduate higher education. The proposal for three echelons of media service— system, building, classroom—had already been described in my book, Instructional Materials, *published by Ronald Press in 1960.*

This morning I want you to forget that I am a librarian. Instead, I want you to think of me as a new superintendent taking over in a new sixty-eighth Florida county, carved out of a large county that needs dividing.

I am young, with a fresh Ph.D. There is a fervor to do something about the national unrest over our schools. Although I am not convinced that our American education is a failure, or that Johnny can't read, or that Mary can't do simple arithmetic, I have a patriotic desire to do better. Not only because I want us to beat the Russians to the moon, but because I sincerely believe that for all our faults and mistakes, our way of life is nearer to His Kingdom than that achieved by any nation of world history.

When I look at American education today, one simple fact impresses me: the ratio between teachers and pupils is steadily becoming more unfavorable. War babies are inundating our classrooms, nationally. But, here in Florida we are adding to that problem with the largest population increase in any state. This tells me that each teacher must teach more pupils. It tells me, even more forcefully, that the national commitment to education for all of the people means that there are more individual differences.

In the course of my Ph.D. work at the university, I have examined many solutions, both historical and current. One idea that remains in my thinking comes from the English educator Joseph Lancaster (1778-1838). He developed the monitorial system of instruction suggested by Andrew Bell (1753-1832)—namely, the idea of using older students as monitors to drill the younger ones in fundamentals. It was revived by the current efforts of Dr. Laubach's "each one teach one" program for eliminating illiteracy in the world. Another current development, in Norwalk, Connecticut, called team teaching, also stirred me, but not as an extension into the elementary grades of secondary school departmentalized learning.

Instead, both the historical monitor and the current team teacher accented for me the basic solution: individual differences in pupils must be matched by individual differences in materials. What weakened the old Lancasterian attempt was the lack of quantity and variety of materials. What makes the current Norwalk team teaching program so promising is its heavy reliance on materials—many materials, covering the whole range and variety of formats. Where the Norwalk plan still needs strengthening, in my perhaps superficial view of it, is in the concept of coordination.

Every team needs a team leader. The sharing of teaching responsibility

A paper read before a conference at Florida Agricultural and Mechanical University, Tallahassee, October 19, 1962.

among two or more teachers promises distinct advantages over the "self-contained" classroom. The former offers the efficiency of specialization, but it carries also the hazard of compartmentalization, unless there is a coordinating, unifying influence. As a Ph.D. student, the coordination, the team leadership seemed ready-made for our schools. Horace Mann, in the early nineteenth century, had conceived of the school library as the coordinating instructional unit of the school. At the turn of the twentieth century, the late, great Dr. William Torey Harris (who, as Superintendent of St. Louis public schools, fathered both school libraries and the earliest aspects of audiovisual education) declared, when he was U.S. Commissioner of Education: "Inevitably, our schools are tending toward making school library material the central learning effort of our education."

As I assumed responsibility for my "sixty-eighth county" school system, I was aware of the obstacles to a library-centered school. First, personnel. Too many principals still looked upon the library as an accessory to the classroom. Too many teachers used the library inadequately, if at all. Too many pupils were unable to use a library for a variety of reasons.

If I seem to place the pupils third in that series, let me say immediately that they are first in all of our educational consideration. This is the punch line, as you know. The conference participant who gets in the words "but the children come first" frequently gets a burst of applause. I hope such demagoguery will not survive much longer. I'm sure this clincher must give way to the assumption that all of us who have foregone more lucrative opportunities put the children first. We merely differ on how best to serve the children.

But, in addition to the principal, the teacher and the pupil, the librarian himself, in many instances, has not understood his potential. He has too often looked upon himself as a technician—one who glories in classifying and cataloging his books, in maintaining a proper charging system, or perhaps in dispatching book orders. In addition, he too frequently has reservations about certain classes of materials—those called audiovisual.

My first move as "superintendent" was, therefore, to find personnel willing to plan a truly library-centered school. I began with a supervisor. Call this supervisor general coordinator or instructional materials coordinator. The supervisor has demonstrated in his undergraduate work that he learns better in the library than he does in the conventional classroom. He has overcome the great neglect in teacher education of instructional materials, of always studying them incidentally, and never *per se*. He is committed to no single format over all others. Hardcover books, or celluloid films, have no prescriptive rights over the less dramatized media. To him, they are all part of the educational mission to augment communication between teacher and pupil.

Preferably, this instructional materials coordinator is a graduate of an accredited library school, in addition to being a college graduate, and a certified teacher. He might conceivably have the doctorate based on both teacher and library education. Such programs are advancing in our graduate education, cooperatively planned by schools of education and library schools on university campuses such as Columbia, Illinois, and Florida State.

To assist him, I advise a full-time professional librarian for each building—elementary as well as junior and senior high school. In addition, I confirm professional library staff at the system level, for central acquisition, processing, dissemination, and reference.

There is a smile of approval on my face when the supervisor resists two deputies—one for library, one for AV. Says my supervisor, "This is too artificial. I don't know where one begins and one leaves off. Give me two deputy supervisors, but let one be for elementary, the other for secondary, and let both be responsible in their respective level for the whole range of materials." For the very large high school he maintains the same philosophy.

"We will need three librarians at Central High," says he, "but please do not designate one of them as 'audiovisual.' I want all three to know all kinds of materials. I may divide their assignments: one, social sciences; another, language arts; a third, science."

The supervisor now is startled when I say, "I want two aides for every professional librarian you employ. There must be no waste of professional time on clerical duties. If we are going to demonstrate that children can learn better through library-learning, then the librarian must be free to plan, innovate, create."

And while we are on personnel, the supervisor and I agree that some teacher mis-education will have to be redone. Principals and teachers will need to know materials better than they now do. They will need to learn the formats they don't know, and to understand better the potentials and limitations of the ones they do know.

As we look at the universe of materials today, at least a hundred different forms and formats are available in our nation's schools. I offer you this broad format classification of what we now call "educational media." There are, of course, many sub-classes.

THE GENERIC BOOK: SIX FORMAT CLASSES

I. Print	IV. Transmissions
II. Graphics	V. Community Resources
III. Projections	VI. Programmed Media

To organize these parts of the generic book for most effective communication between teacher and pupil, three echelons of service are proposed for my sixty-eighth county. These are designated: 1) system center; 2) building center; 3) classroom center.

SYSTEM ECHELON

To provide ultimate coordination for materials teamwork, the system center is located in the same unit as the superintendent's administrative offices. It is administered by the supervisor and his headquarters staff of deputies, specialists and aides. Committees of librarians, teachers, and principals participate in policy making.

A central acquisitions unit orders, for the entire system, all materials and equipment, including books, periodicals, other print, films (both purchase and rental), etc. A union catalog of all holdings in materials and equipment provides control, especially on large and expensive items for which duplication may be unnecessary.

To serve all teaching and administrative personnel, the system center maintains a professional library, including curriculum materials, courses of study, books and journals in education, psychology, library science, and audiovisual instruction. Reference service on these is offered by phone as well as on the scene.

Reservoirs are maintained of expensive materials, including encyclopedia sets, films, and other materials that are too expensive for any one school budget and that can be shared. Here, then, at the system level, is the hub of the materials network.

BUILDING ECHELON

At the building echelon there is a model library of the Florida materials center type. The proposed unit for each ADA 500 has already been achieved, or better, plus at least one aide for each professional. If two or more librarians are provided, division of labor is not by format, but by subject or level.

The materials represent teamwork selection by teachers, librarians, and students. For each subject area and level, recommendations are made by individual teachers, and correlated by the librarian. To insure continuous scrutiny of new materials, a bibliographic exchange is coordinated in the library. At least monthly, a teacher's meeting is devoted to review, not only of print, but of projections, transmissions, etc.

The center itself, centrally located (possibly on the ground floor, if community service is provided as well), is not only amply lighted, but is adequately treated for sound and projection. Conference rooms are numerous, for teachers alone and for pupils.

CLASSROOM ECHELON

The school library as materials center begins and ends at the classroom echelon. All of the trends in tomorrow's school point to learning through materials. A look at modern teaching suggests at once that the teacher must be prepared to perform as a librarian in her classroom in at least these three ways: 1) selection of materials and equipment; 2) organization of these to facilitate use; 3) utilization of them to communicate even more effectively to the individual differences among her pupils.

I am not unaware that the mere mention of classroom libraries suggests hazards. But not if we understand the theme of this conference. Teamwork does not allow the proprietary intolerance over a classroom collection that we formerly associated with extreme decentralization. As understood here, classroom libraries are the third echelon of a team effort to learn through instructional materials.

It is my hope that if the proposal for earmarked instructional materials funds goes through, along with the library unit for every 500 ADA, it will be possible for every classroom in our schools to have a library consisting of two parts. One part would be the permanent equipment and collection of materials. I will not enumerate this classroom core here, but it will certainly include more than the chalkboard. It could well include an overhead projector, a tape recorder, a disc listening post, and possibly slide and opaque projectors.

Materials begin with the textbook adoptions and include basic reference books for that grade–dictionary, encyclopedia, atlas. Permanent belongings should be a 12-inch terrestrial globe, and possibly a celestial globe in some rooms, augmented by a basic wall map collection.

There should be at least one vertical file, filled with exciting pictures, transparencies, charts, and ephemeral print. Objects, including specimens, are creatively represented. Nor are bulletin boards, exhibits, and dioramas forgotten. Permanent as these collections are for the classroom, a central inventory belongs in the building center; and no teacher, I hope, would ever be so professionally selfish as not to lend through this library system.

The rotating classroom collection will change with study units. To both teacher and pupil, the selection challenge will constitute the essence of learning.

We have overcome the obstacles of personnel, materials, and organization, presumably. What are the obstacles to library learning?

Librarian leadership must first assume a more dynamic role. We must forget our perpetual ancillary complex. Not only does selection follow the curriculum, but the curriculum follows selection.

Consider that man's best is in the media–his greatest deeds, his most beautiful creations, his finest ideas. Consider also that the high mission of librarianship is the dissemination of our best achievements. How can we who evaluate and select from among all the records of civilization escape our responsibility for shaping the curriculum at every level and age, from birth to death. That we have hung back and have let the curriculum be developed for us by others is not to our credit.

As the new superintendent of System 68 in Florida, I have designs for a new teamwork. The team will be truly library-centered, with a new breed of faculty and student who learn and teach with media. In this new teamwork the student studies independently under the bibliographic guidance of the faculty. The curriculum is a composite of faculty syllabi and student interest profiles. And the library, reflecting the individual difference of School System 68, is the kind of learning resource center that is committed to selection of the generic book.

THE LIBRARY-CENTERED SCHOOL

A forerunner of the medium school is this dream of a school that is essentially a library, a school in which the librarian leads, rather than follows, both in curriculum development and in new dimensions of learning. This dream predicts the passing of the classroom as we have known it, and without classrooms to "support," the librarian is free to show a better way to elementary and secondary education.

Experimenting schools and colleges today are relentlessly shifting the learning locus from classroom to library. If there is one dominating, dramatic trend in American education, it is the trend to independent study.

At the very top of our educational structure, Harvard has announced that medical students, in revolt against the classroom-lecture mode of teaching, would be permitted to substitute library learning at their individual pace. For at least three decades now, an increasing number of liberal arts colleges have been replacing classroom attendance with something variously labelled "honors reading," "autonomous courses," "tutorial system," or "preceptorial plan." Each year Florida Presbyterian suspends classes during the whole month of January, so that all students can study independently in the library. Among junior colleges, Stephens in Missouri has long fostered independent study through what the former dean, who also served as the librarian, called "the vitalized library." At Wakulla Springs, Florida, in a unique symposium, ten experimenting colleges reported on variations of the independent study idea.[1] The library implications are simply revolutionary.

Evidences of an independent study trend in secondary and even elementary education are cascading daily. Contributing to the *Bulletin* of the National Association of Secondary School Principals, issued in January 1966,[2] a school superintendent, a principal, and a librarian all attest to the mounting force of the independent study movement. In the superintendent's words: ". . . the school library can be considered the pulse of the instructional program . . ." and therefore, as the school system's chief administrative officer, he considers it his duty to encourage the principals under him to discover the library's new educational role.

But the principal who contributes to this monumental symposium has already anticipated all that the superintendent has in mind by his appraisal: "One of the more significant criticisms of secondary schools by college faculty has been that many high school graduates do not know how to use library resources effectively. . . . Teaching students advanced library skills undoubtedly is one of the more important curriculum tasks of the faculty. . . ."[3]

Too often, we must admit, the librarian has been so involved with the means that the ends have escaped most, if not all, of our attention. That this is not so in the case of the librarian contributor is nowhere more evident than

Based on a paper read to the California School Library Association, San Francisco, March 1965.

in her observation: "The key concept in many scheduling and curriculum innovations is independent study."[4]

Why this must become increasingly so is underlined not by a librarian but by a school of education dean:

> The emerging image of the school is still blurred, but some of the ways in which it will depart from current practice are discernible. It will focus on learning rather than teaching, and use teaching not so much to impart knowledge as to stimulate and guide learning ... bring together a large variety of inducements to and resources for learning .. create situations through which learning progress can be motivated, systematized, and appraised as far as possible on an individual basis.[5]

"On an individual basis." Therein lies the prime motivation for the current trend to independent study. Another school superintendent has expressed the drive behind this inevitable objective in a nation committed to educating all of the people regardless of how widely divergent the talents of each person:

> ... today the majority of our classrooms are organized in heterogeneous groups with little more than a courteous nod to the wide range of differences in each group ... although the facts of individual differences are startling and have been well known since 1900, with the work of Binet and his followers on the measure of intellectual capacity.[6]

It must be apparent that at the heart of American educational experimenting is the effort to tailor education to the widening range of individual differences caused by universal schooling. It must be equally obvious that experimenting colleges and universities are moving out of the group teaching focus of the classroom to the individual learning mode of the library. Already at least one college, Jamestown in North Dakota, will activate a library-college in which learning will be centered in the library. Secondary schools like Ridgewood in Norridge, Illinois, and elementary schools like those in Shaker Heights, Ohio, have experimented so far in independent study that there is considerable promise that our schools of the near future will be library-centered in a sense we have never meant before.

THE LEARNING MODE OF THE LIBRARY-CENTERED SCHOOL

The library-centered school accepts individual learning rather than group teaching. It can be said to reverse the traditional relationship between classroom and library by requiring the pupil to read, view, and listen more in the library while the teacher provides bibliographic guidance beforehand, then counsels, confers, and evaluates on an individual basis. The learning mode can be illustrated by the three stages reported for independent study at the Ridgewood High School. In stage one the pupil works on short assignments planned by the teacher under close supervision. Stage two is characterized by longer projects, but these, too, are pre-planned by the teacher. When the student is ready for full independent study, he enters stage three, where the project is of his own planning.

In this mode of learning the pupil moves steadily toward independence in learning. Let it be noted that this independent study is not intended as the exclusive right of the gifted child. On the contrary, the very nature of independent study permits recognition of individual differences the way group teaching in the classroom mode prohibits it. To accomplish independent study as a learning mode the school must be library-centered in fact as well as in sentiment. The school library must become, as my colleague Sara Srygley says, the "intellectual laboratory designed for teaching and learning the process of free inquiry."[7]

THE LIBRARY-CENTERED SCHOOL LIBRARY

Call it materials center, or instructional materials center, or learning resources laboratory, or any other name that you think will enlist more exciting involvement by funding sources, by administrators, by teachers, and above all by pupils. The fact remains that the materials center we pioneered in Florida, in spite of any subsequent relabellings, is basically a library. But the materials center is a library that is willing to break with certain stereotypes that have tended to create a superficial image of the librarian and a subordinate role for the library in the learning process.

The materials center concept differs from the traditional library in the idea of what a book is, in the organization of the collection of books, in the place of the book in the learning process, and especially in the relationship of teacher, librarian, and student to the book.

To begin with, in the materials center the book is what I call the "generic book," encompassing all of the formats from textbook through television and computerized learning consoles. Materials are now so many, and are so varied in format, content, and level, that for the first time in the history of education we can match individual differences in children and young people with individual differences in learning materials. During the last year alone the 30,000 new book titles published in the United States were supplemented by thousands of magazine articles, countless films, filmstrips, transparencies, discs, tapes, radio and TV programs, revelations of community resources—to say nothing of the millions of media produced abroad or in the years preceding.

To help you understand something of the range of media that constitute the generic book, I offer you a format classification (see page 50) of the different media or materials—the generic book—found in the libraries and audiovisual centers of our nation's schools. There is another element in the concept of the materials center. In its true form it recognizes no line between the so-called audiovisual and other materials. In the true materials center the generic book is a continuum. There is no way the librarian can separate by using a term that has become obnoxious in Florida materials centers, "non-book materials." Nor can the audiovisualist separate so-called library materials from films or tapes or anything else he might consider "audiovisual." The reason is that they are all media, all instructional materials.

As proof of this all one has to do is pick up a book on audiovisual materials, like the fine text by Wittich and Schuller, and a book on library book selection like *Children's Catalog* and the *Standard Catalog for High School Libraries*. It is at once evident that the professional librarian and audiovisualist both concern themselves with the selection of maps and globes. Both devote considerable attention to pictures, although audiovisual terminology designates them as "flat." For years librarians have collected and exhibited various specimens, models, and objects of all kinds; although some AV texts fancily designate these things as "realia," they are no different as a format class. As early as 1928 the Carnegie Corporation gave a million dollars worth of selected phonograph recordings to U.S. libraries. Subsequently, this format was designated "phonodisc" by the Library of Congress and just "disc" by audiovisualists. Transparencies and overhead projectors have long been one of my favorite classroom teaching media. Largely because of my educational belief in this format, I influenced my publisher to be among the first to include transparency overlays in the encyclopedia I edit.

If what I have said thus far appears to underestimate audiovisual contributions, let me recall that I offered the first audiovisual course to librarians and teachers in the South at Peabody as early as 1935. The library school I now head is the first ALA-accredited school to require audiovisual competence of all of its graduates. For all the years following World War II, I worked unceasingly to enact and implement our unique unified certification in Instructional Materials, which is parenthesized as "library-audiovisual." Because of my almost passionate belief in audiovisual materials and the tremendous impact the audiovisual movement has had not only on libraries but on education, I have carried on a personal crusade in both DAVI and ALA to unite our forces with the aim of bringing about a better education. Some will recall the *NEA Journal* forum as well as the *Educational Screen* in which I championed the unity concept that is the foundation of the true materials center. The idea of having a library at one end of the school building and an audiovisual center at the other has always seemed to me much less desirable. I can't imagine the teacher asking, "Was the globe you consulted an audiovisual globe or a library globe?," when they are one and the same. But I can see indecision on the part of the teacher and pupils as to which of the two separate centers to go to for certain formats. First of all, then, the materials center is exactly what the Pennsylvania Department of Public Instruction curriculum development manual calls it: "A centrally located area of the school building through which the selection, purchase or production, distribution, maintenance and storage of all types of instructional materials is accomplished."[8]

MATERIALS CENTER ORGANIZATION

Organizationally, I have described the materials center for a school system as consisting of three echelons. The middle echelon, or building center, is the unit most often identified with the term materials center or school library. As found in most high schools today and eventually in all secondary and elementary schools, it most nearly meets the Pennsylvania definition. The building materials center directs the selection, acquisition and dissemination of all formats of instructional materials for all studies and levels. It is tending to give up most of its organizing of materials to a central processing unit. The building materials center houses all materials and equipment for the school and maintains an inventory in at least two and usually three record forms, consisting of a shelf list, a public catalog, and frequently a separate accession book, which is coming back with the aroused interest in library history.

The top echelon materials center is at the system level. In Florida we have only county school systems, but the same pattern can apply in city systems, as it does in places like Rochester, New York, and Portland, Oregon. System centers at their best have a number of coordinating units for all of the schools, including central acquisition or ordering of all materials. Our largest counties, like Dade and Broward, will frequently order 200 or more copies of the same title for upward of 100 schools in the system; this is advantageous discount business efficiency. Central processing of these materials for all of the schools is steadily coming. Indeed, in Hawaii the state library provides central processing for all public as well as school libraries in the state. Not only is it more economical and efficient, but it frees the time of librarians at the building level for the main business of working with pupils and teachers. With the coming of computerized printout catalogs, even more exciting central processing developments are in store. For example, our information science professor is exploring with our 30 public junior college libraries the feasibility of a CPC that will acquire, classify, and catalog materials for all of the libraries centrally, furnishing printout book catalogs in quantity, continuously updated and reproduced in any desired quantity, plus an unlimited number of bibliographies on individual study units. The system center maintains a union catalog of all the school libraries.

The system center also has a library with several components. First of all, it houses those materials that are too expensive to purchase for the exclusive use of any one school and that are shared by all. The film library is an example of this. Infrequently used expensive sets of books and journals are other examples, as well as support duplicates.

The curriculum laboratory or the curriculum library, if we are mindful of the difference indicated in the professional literature, is another component. Here are housed the teachers' professional library, textbooks in and out of adoption, courses of study, teaching units, lesson plans, and other sections. The impact of such a component on curriculum development in a school system is directly related to whether its role is active or passive.

We call our production component the "graphics laboratory." Here instructional materials are created and constructed. From the systems level graphics laboratory much direction is given to the graphics efforts both at the building and at the classroom level. In 1949 we introduced a graphics course for librarians and teachers into our library school curriculum. In that laboratory I have seen ideas developed for instructional materials ranging from chalkboard tracing patterns and templates to striking picture dry mounts, to dioramas, murals, posters, startling ideas for peg, flannel and magnetic boards, transparency overlays, slides, filmstrips, tapes, motion pictures, radio transcriptions, TV kinescopes, and programmed learning.

On the system level the coordination is directed by a materials supervisor or coordinator. One of our Florida counties once decided to call him "Supervisor of Multi-sensory Materials." I shall never forget the slip I made at a professional meeting where I had to introduce him. As a devotee of J. B. Rhine at Duke, with a growing conviction that parapsychology is adding a new dimension to our understanding of learning, I introduced him as the supervisor of extra-sensory materials.

In some of our counties, like Dade, there are two assistant supervisors of school libraries and of audiovisual materials. Sometimes a third assistant supervisor of television is added. Variations of this pattern are found, as in our state department, where the curriculum specialist is the overall supervisor. A variation tried in Houston expresses the unity concept of materials better than any other. The functions of the assistant supervisors are divided not by format but by level. One assistant supervisor has charge of the whole range of materials for the elementary level, and the other for the secondary level. This departure has been frequently paralleled on the building level by a division of function by subject matter. Instead of designating one member of the high school library staff as audiovisual, each of three staff members has been given responsibility, respectively, for science materials, for social studies, for language arts.

As the instructional materials program grows, provision for format specialists may be in order. Some of the most frequent specialties are classification and cataloging, reference and information, radio and television, motion picture and photographic production, and more recently automation and computerized learning.

The ultimate consumers are in the third echelon, at the classroom level. In the library-centered school committed to the independent study idea, the present classroom group teaching rooms are beginning to look each day more like individualized library learning centers. Inevitably, tomorrow's classroom, and in some cases today's, will look more like a library than a classroom. It will be well stocked with books. About half of these will be permanently located in that room. The permanent materials will consist of at least one general encyclopedia on the appropriate level, several dictionaries and atlases, a selection of maps, two globes (one terrestrial and the other, now more than ever, celestial, since we shall be on the moon this decade and on more distant planets in the lifetime of the generation we now teach).

The other half will be a changing collection of materials borrowed from the building materials center and related to the several studies and projects of the individual pupils. Basic room equipment for the use of materials may include opaque, overhead, slide, and filmstrip projectors, or a combination of them, closed circuit access to building transmissions, radio and TV sets, tape recorder and disc playback.

If there is still any reluctance among us about classroom libraries, let us read what Dr. Jean Lowrie writes:

> It is unfortunate . . . that many elementary-school librarians or teacher-librarians retain too tight a control of the library materials. The fear of wide circulation of materials outside the library or of the development of the autonomous classroom collection rather than the fluctuating collection has deterred the program in elementary-school library service.[9]

THE LIBRARY FACILITY

Housing the materials center was an early concern of ours in Florida. Two of our state department publications are specifically about planning quarters and equipment. Out of our Florida planning developed several considerations supplementary to those usually considered in library planning.

For instance, library architecture has always been obviously concerned about proper lighting for reading. With viewing and auding (the fancy term for listening) becoming ever more critical because of the widening range of materials, more and different provisions for darkening and acoustics were required. In our relatively mild climates of Florida and California the architectural inclination to light and to open-air reading rooms posed problems for daylight projecting. Similarly, as tapes, disc, radio and TV became increasingly a part of something called the "cross media approach," we introduced the listening post into our reading rooms. The listening post consists of a three-speed record player, a multiple phone, and up to eight sets of earphones, so students can sit in the reading room, read *Hamlet*, and listen to John Gielgud play the part.

The systematic procedure of the librarian in developing requirements for a library job to be designed by an architect is to provide three types of accommodations: for materials, for users, for staff. The materials center concept changes library specifications so that accommodation for media other than the hardcover book are no longer minor. Essential now are specifications for storage of projectors, recorders, radio and TV sets, as well as for racks to accommodate maps, globes, dioramas, models, exhibits, and storage for filmstrips, slides, tapes, discs, films, and more.

As the school moves to independent study as the mode of learning, individual study spaces become paramount. Current standards, which allow for seating 15 to 30 percent of the student body at one time in the building center, may have to be modified until the day when our classrooms have been fully converted to libraries or materials centers.

A prediction of things to come is found in *Planning Schools for New Media*,[10] prepared by three educators (one of whom was Amo DeBernardis of Portland, Oregon) and and architect, under a contract with the U.S. Office of Education. It suggests four types of user accommodation that libraries are increasingly recognizing in their architectural planning. First of all, individual study spaces. Now libraries have had carrels for a very long time. Indeed, the Ford Foundation Educational Facilities Laboratory has published a whole pamphlet on their design, illustrating some 16 patterns. Second, individual and group listening stations are suggested, well ventilated and convenient for visual supervision. Third, there should be small group conference areas, each to accommodate six to eight students, for discussions or planning meetings. The dual requirement of listening equipment and direct access to reference books poses an acoustics problem. Fourth is the challenge of providing a film preview space for use by small groups, equipped with two or more screens, projectors, and earphones to enable simultaneous previewing of two or more films. And fifth, microfilm reader space is sketched that promises more convenience than that allowed by the ordinary casual provisions.

There are other stimulating hints and ideas for accommodating users, materials, and staff, but since the accent is on newer media, it would be well to consult, along with DeBernardis' guide, another U.S.O.E. release, *Library Facilities for Elementary and Secondary Schools* (1965). The latter is more conventional but gives considerable attention to listening and viewing areas as well as to audiovisual storage and graphics production. The furniture and equipment section provides key specifications.

STUDENT, TEACHER, LIBRARIAN RELATIONS

The tangible considerations of materials, organization, and facilities have always been easier for us because our national talent is for the pragmatic. When it comes to the intangible our pragmatics carry over into something we show off as the scientific method. Perhaps education is or can be made a science. In our weaker moments, perhaps, we concede that the great teacher and good learning are arts.

The library-centered school with independent study as a mode can, I believe, prove superior to the present classroom-centered school with group teaching as a mode, simply through reformation of the range, organization, and facilities of materials. But the library-centered school can approach its ultimate potential only as the new generation fully reorients itself.

For students this orientation will be easiest of all, not only because their youth gives them greater flexibility and readiness for change, but because they have been revolting against an instructional system dating from an age when media were few and inadequate to meet individual differences and instruction had to be carried on in groups by word of mouth from the master.

The orientation will be slower with us, the older generation of teachers, librarians, and administrators. As teachers we were educated in schools of education where instructional materials, when they were taught at all, were taught incidentally, rarely *per se*. Our professors explained this not for the real reason that their generation had never been properly taught the use of libraries and their materials, but on the grounds that it was more meaningful to teach materials in relation to subjects, to method, to curriculum development, to supervision, to administration, to elementary or secondary education, to child or adolescent psychology. But one day I asked a colleague at Peabody, "Suppose we were to reverse it and teach all of those things incidentally to materials. What would that do to teacher education?" Strangely enough he paused, pondered thoughtfully, and then for months after kept bringing this idea up every time he saw me, with the conclusion that a teacher education agency somewhere sometime ought to try it.

We do much better now. All teacher education agencies offer courses in children's and young people's literature, in audiovisual instruction, in library use, and in elementary library science. Some states, like Florida, require that all elementary teachers have a basic course in instructional materials. Our secondary teachers have not yet gained a similar requirement.

But if our teacher education has not yet committed itself sufficiently to media education for our teachers-in-preparation, an increasing number of teachers-in-service are undertaking to study the universe of educational media on their own so that they may know the strengths and weaknesses of each format in relation to individual learning situations. Furthermore, they are studying content and level so that they may screen more expertly from the annual output of some 50,000 new items, the few most needed in their working relations with pupils and colleagues and in their own self-improvement.

As librarians we also know our professional education has been far from perfect. Blame me as much as any, because I now have the questionable distinction of having served longest as head of an ALA-accredited library school. But, God knows, I have tried to reform library education for almost all of my 36 years in it. My audiovisual efforts bore some fruit. But progress in reforming and reaccenting our role in education and research is confronted by a professional ancillary complex. In research we insist on retrieval rather than synthesis and interpretation of information. In education our highest aim is to support classroom instruction rather than to guide independent learning.

The hope lies in our new generation of librarians. Each year in my classes they seem more willing to study library practice not only as it is today but as it might be. Consequently, the school librarians of our new generation are willing to follow the curriculum and supply readings for it, but they are even more anxious to have a hand in developing the curriculum out of their rich knowledge of materials. They are not only ready to support the classroom teacher but anxious to share in the learning process by converting both pupils and classroom teachers to independent library learning.

Inevitably classroom teachers will become as bibliographically competent as librarians, and librarians as pedagogically qualified and committed as classroom teachers, with the good possibility that a new breed of school faculty will emerge—a cross between the best in classroom teaching and the best in librarianship.

As that day approaches, the library-centered school seems nearer to reality. When that day comes, our children and young people will have the opportunity to match their individual differences with an independent learning program.

FOOTNOTES

1. W. Hugh Stickler, ed., *Experimental Colleges: Their Role in American Higher Education* (Tallahassee, Florida State University, 1964).

2. "Libraries in Secondary School: A New Look," National Association of Secondary School Principals. *Bulletin*, No. 306 (January 1966).

3. H. O. Elseroad, "The Superintendent's Key Role," *ibid.*, p. 1.

4. G. L. Schwilk, "The Library Needs the Principal," *ibid.*, p. 9.

5. Margaret H. Grazier, "The Library's New Programs," *ibid.*, p. 22.

6. F. S. Chase, "America Evaluates Its Schools," in *New Definitions of School Library Service*, ed. by Sara Innis Fenwick. University of Chicago Graduate Library School, 24th Conference (Chicago, University of Chicago Press, 1960), p. 7.

7. K. W. Lund, in *New Definitions of School Library Service*, p. 13.

8. Sara K. Srygley, "A New Look at the Older Media," National Association of Secondary School Principals. *Bulletin*, No. 306 (January 1966), p. 26.

9. Jean Lowrie, "Elementary School Libraries Today," in *New Definitions of School Library Service*, pp. 27-28.

10. Amo DeBernardis, *et al.*, *Planning Schools for New Media* (Portland, Oregon, Portland State College, 1961).

THE MEDIUM SCHOOL

*By 2000 A.D., the library will have replaced the classroom.
Because teaching and learning will be primarily through the wide
range of media formats, levels and subjects that are increasingly
available, the education process will have become basically the
sensitive matching by the teacher of individual differences in
students with individual differences in media. As a result the
present classroom-centered school will have become a medium
school.*

Thirty-three years from today we will be in the year 2000. We can no
longer talk about the Buck Rogers century as something out of our world.
Many of the unbelievables from science fiction, including an imminent visit to
the moon, are already here. What these next 33 years will bring to the world
is still speculative in most areas, and education is probably no exception.
Nevertheless, it pays to look ahead and conjecture.

By the year 2000 the library will replace the classroom as the center of
learning. Students of all ages, from kindergarten through graduate school, will
be independently studying, at an individual pace, increasingly varied and
exciting instructional materials. Guidance will come from a new breed of
teacher, a cross between those who today teach in classrooms and those who
teach in libraries. The curriculum will follow the library rather than vice
versa, as is currently accepted. Sacred specialties of today will give way to
increasingly interdisciplinary approaches to knowledge. The school facility
will be essentially a library. These are the broad outlines of what I foresee as
the "medium school" of the twenty-first century.

Medium as defined by the dictionary is "anything that serves or acts
intermediately . . . a channel . . . an intervening instrumentation . . . a sur-
rounding or enveloping element or substance . . . a condition of life."[1] The
medium school "serves or acts intermediately" between learner and environment.

THE PASSING OF THE CLASSROOM

Traditionally the classroom has been the symbol of instruction, where
students of all ages and of varying backgrounds have been taught by a master.
Instruction has been oral-lecture, recitation, discussion, and report, increasingly supplemented by visual communication—from chalkboard through
projection. Textbook assignments have expanded from reserve assignments of
specific pages of a restricted number of books to unlimited browsing. A few
experimenting colleges, and even fewer experimental schools, have released
superior students from class attendance for something now variously called
independent study, honors reading, or autonomous courses. In this trend
toward individual, independent study can be found the embryo of the

Reprinted with permission from the *Phi Delta Kappan*, 48:285-88 (February 1967).

learning mode that characterizes the medium school.

Speaking before the 24th annual conference of the University of Chicago Graduate Library School, School Superintendent Kenneth W. Lund of Oak Park, Illinois, observed, "Today the majority of our classrooms are organized into heterogeneous groups with little more than a courteous nod to the wide range of difference in each group. . . . The facts of individual differences are startling and have been well known since 1900, with the work of Binet and his followers on the measure of intellectual capacity."[2] This puts the finger on the inherent weakness of classroom group teaching as the dominant learning mode. Individual differences can be accommodated most imperfectly in a lesson plan that must aim for a mythical average in an ever-widening range, as we approach our national goal of universal education.

The failure of the classroom to provide adequately for individual differences is only half of its essential weakness as a learning mode. The other half relates to its accent on teaching rather than learning. Commenting on the "emerging image of the school" and "some of the ways in which it will depart from current practice," the dean of the University of Chicago Graduate School of Education predicts that the school of the future "will focus on learning rather than teaching and use teaching not so much to impart knowledge as to stimulate and guide learning."[3]

Already many classrooms are becoming libraries, and classroom teachers true librarians, as the class period becomes essentially a book-reading, or film-viewing, or tape-auding session, under the guidance of a bibliographically competent teacher. Each student works at his own pace with a medium tailored to his individual aptitude and preparation, seeking such individual conference or group instruction as his own effort requires for supplement.

LIBRARY STUDENTS

Heretofore it has been assumed that independent study or honors reading is only for the so-called "gifted" student. The medium school assumes that all children are gifted, some with one talent, some with others. It is up to the school to help each child discover and develop his individual talents, and surround these special talents with adequate general competence for him to live in his environment. The medium school proposes to do this by matching individual differences in learners with individual approaches to learning through a variety of media. Because of the great number and wide range of educational media now available, it is possible to match individual differences in children with individual differences in media.

LIBRARY TEACHERS

Obviously, this mode of learning will require a new generation of classroom and library teachers. But this new generation will be able to point to its genesis in the library-minded teachers and teaching-minded librarians of today's schools.

It requires no intensive search to discover classroom teachers in great number today who are teaching social sciences and language arts largely through reading guidance. In the classrooms of these teachers are found well-selected collections of materials; some of these are personal possessions of the teacher, some belong to the class, and a greater number are borrowed from the school library.

Nor does it require any search to discover school librarians far more interested in reference and reading guidance with students than in processing materials. The trend toward central processing is helping these teaching-minded librarians. But even without central processing, these librarians are more than ever freeing themselves from housekeeping routines to devote their efforts primarily to the true and high role of librarianship, which is to stimulate and guide learning.

Inevitably, library-minded classroom teachers and teaching-minded librarians will merge their efforts and assume their rightful role in an independent, individual, library-centered learning mode.

LIBRARY CURRICULUM

The former president of Stanford University, Ray Lyman Wilbur, has been quoted (although not always credited) as saying, "Changing the curriculum is like moving a cemetery. No matter how long what's there has been dead, it still has a lot of friends."

Yet the curriculum must change. If many agree on this, more differ on how. Some favor a return to the so-called "tough subjects," i.e., math, science, foreign languages, English, history, and certain other disciplines. Others advocate more attention to living and to personal adjustment.

A library curriculum for the medium school suggests that we reverse the usual development procedures of first constructing a course of study and then selecting materials to communicate it. A library curriculum for the medium school would begin with book selection, or media selection, if the term medium is not identified as the generic book. The medium school's curriculum would be developed on the foundation of a well-selected library. The assumption is that the best of human experiences, actions, and thoughts are included in the record of civilization.

The second principle of the library curriculum is to assume that knowledge is unified and to recognize no artificial boundaries or rights among predatory so-called subjects, tough or otherwise.

Recognizing the opposing trend toward generalism in a world of increasing specialism would be a third principle in library curriculum development. This is a natural tendency of general librarianship, which has always served all of the subjects impartially. Consequently, the library and librarianship can contribute something like an interdisciplinary *gestalt* to curriculum development. Moreover, there is an opportunity for serendipity, of which research has made so much lately.

Further, if the half of knowledge is, as the oft-quoted statement declares, "knowing where to find it," then librarianship, which has devoted itself to the study of sources *per se*, has a content as well as a method to contribute to the curriculum.

THE MEDIUM SCHOOL LIBRARY

I have no objection to renaming the fourth element of the medium school—the library—a "learning center." Perhaps we in Florida have been among the first to relabel our school libraries "materials centers." Our certification for both librarians and audiovisualists in Florida has, for nearly 15 years now, been designated "instructional materials." We had a shotgun marriage of the two professional groups, librarians and audiovisualists, some years ago, and part of the compromise was to rename the library. We had a more difficult time renaming the librarian. Since neither materialist nor medium, rakishly suggested during the great professional debate, quite described our merged profession, we ended up with *instructional materials specialist*, or librarian. But there is no question about the greater dramatic effect, especially in money-getting, of some label fancier than "library."

For years before the birth of the audiovisual movement, of course, libraries disseminated maps and globes, pictures (though we didn't call them "flats"), museum objects (which we didn't describe as "realia"), and records (that are audiovisually labeled "discs"). We gloried in our bulletin boards, posters, murals, and diagrams (but we didn't call them graphics).

On the other hand, we know that the audiovisual movement stirred librarianship to reexamine its repugnance toward formats other than the hard cover.

It was AV that reawakened our desire to participate actively instead of passively in the learning process. Audiovisualists, too, revised library management concepts and introduced new ideas for housing all types of media. Audiovisualists first made librarians aware that darkening was as important as lighting, and that acoustics are an element of new significance in facility planning.

Accumulating all of the influences of traditional and current librarianship, of audiovisualism, automation, and the computer era, a medium school library for the twenty-first century emerges. It is apparent that selection will not be limited by format, subject, or even level, since the range of pupil talents will become even wider with the realization of truly universal education. The processing of these media will inevitably be done centrally, at the system level, and in some instances by a state or even a federal agency. Library of Congress and Wilson cards are current examples of central processing on a national scale. The Hawaii State Library's central processing for school as well as public libraries is an example of state-wide technical processing.

ECHELONS OF SERVICE

As I indicated in my book, *Instructional Materials*,[4] I envisage three echelons of library service within a school system. As now, the building echelon will be key to the whole plan, serving as the central resource center for the individual school. The school library will become the wholesaler for the library rooms, formerly known as classrooms.

The Classroom Echelon. If there are some among us who still have reservations about classroom libraries, I suggest the rereading of Jean Lowrie's article, "Elementary School Libraries Today." "It is unfortunate," Dr. Lowrie writes, "that many elementary-school librarians or teacher-librarians retain too tight a control of the library materials. The fear of wider circulation of materials outside the library, or of the development of the autonomous classroom collection, has deterred the program in the elementary-school library."[5]

In the medium school every classroom will contain a collection of permanently assigned and rotating materials. The former will include such reference tools as selected dictionaries; at least one good encyclopedia set; carefully chosen fact books like almanacs, handbooks, manuals, atlases; wall and desk maps; a globe or two, terrestrial and celestial; several periodicals and newspapers; some pictures, slides, discs, transparencies, tapes, posters, and other display materials. Along with these will be the basic equipment: chalkboard, bulletin board, projecting equipment, playbacks, reviewers, radio, television.

The rotating collection will represent deposits by students and library teachers together, in relation to the unit or subjects under consideration.

The System Echelon. The coordinating library echelon at the system level will perform many functions. In addition to central processing for all schools, the system library will provide a professional collection for teachers and will house expensive parts of the media collection shared by several schools, such as the computer, the telecasting and radio transmission studies, and the film library. Its graphics laboratory for the production of materials will be more extensive, and will supplement the lesser resources of the building center or the classroom library.

But even more significant than its media processing and coordinating activities will be the system library's responsibilities for curriculum and in-service or continuing education. Since media selection precedes curriculum development, the impact of writing, publishing, and media producing will influence the medium school's course of study. Professional currency with the media output will entail even more systematic study of materials than now. In this study the leadership of the system center, and of the supervisor of educational media and his staff, will be of permanent importance.

The shape of the medium school is drawn here only in broad strokes. Dealing in futures is always more hazardous than commentaries on the current scene or retrospection about previous accomplishments. Nevertheless, it is mandatory that our pragmatically inclined nation and profession dream a little about what may come.

Today's trends inevitably predict the medium school of the twenty-first century.

FOOTNOTES

1. *Funk & Wagnalls New Standard Dictionary of the English Language* (New York, Funk & Wagnalls, 1940), p. 1542.

2. K. W. Lund, in *New Definitions of School Library Science*, ed. by Sara Innis Fenwick. University of Chicago Graduate Library School, 24th Conference (Chicago, University of Chicago Press, 1960), p. 13.

3. F. S. Chase, "America Evaluates Its Schools," *ibid.*, p. 7.

4. Louis Shores, *Instructional Materials* (New York, Ronald Press, 1960), pp. 341-62.

5. Jean Lowrie, "Elementary School Libraries Today," in *New Definitions of School Library Science*, pp. 27-28.

PART III:

MEDIA COLLEGE

AUDIOVISUAL DIMENSIONS FOR AN ACADEMIC LIBRARY

Long before Marshall McLuhan suggested the decline of the print medium, Georges Duhamel wrote, in In Defense of Letters *(1939) that the defenseless book would be supplanted by "less laborious methods of information and recreation." Dissenting from the opinions of both Duhamel and McLuhan, I urged my librarian colleagues in colleges and universities, while I was chairman of the ACRL Audio-Visual Committee, to reject this defense complex and to recognize that all formats are part of the generic book. As such, they should be selected and acquired, as well as processed and disseminated, without condescension.*

When a university librarian and a library school dean pause between meetings at a conference, what do they talk about? Usually, of course, about filling that staff vacancy. But almost as frequently these days, about audiovisual (AV) media.

It is no secret that quite a few librarians of institutions of higher education wish that these new-fangled non-book gadgets were somewhere near the bottom of the more unfathomable ocean depths. In the last six months alone I have talked with at least one administrator for every type of academic library represented by our ACRL sections who wished the question of AV media in libraries had never come up. Frankly, they say, in agreement with Joseph Wood Krutch and many other defenders of books, these newer mass media are enemies of reading, and we wonder if our professional responsibility does not call for all-out war. Certainly, the scholarly university library has little reason to cut into its precious research funds for back volumes of the *Berichte der Deutsche Chemische Gesellschaft* in order to buy a half-dozen questionable motion pictures.

Although this position hardly represents the thinking of even a considerable minority of academic librarians, it is worth considering as a starting point for an AV discussion on any campus. For there is considerable fear today that the printed word as a medium of communication may be on the decline. This concern is found not only in the publishing industry, and among writers, but in the profession of librarianship itself. It has already been most fatally predicted by that Frenchman of letters, Georges Duhamel, who wrote as early as 1939:

> The decadence of the book, the greatest instrument for the diffusion of knowledge, may be delayed a little longer. . . . As far as France is concerned the evidence seems to point in one direction. . . . For the man in the street, the book, defenseless, is henceforward to be supplanted by less laborious methods of information and recreation.[1]

Strangely enough the answer to this sort of pessimism comes from an audiovisualist, possibly the foremost audiovisualist in America. Most certainly

Reprinted with permission from *College and Research Libraries*, 15:393-97 (October 1954).

he is the audiovisualist who is authoritatively quoted in research literature in both the AV and the reading fields. In a memorable lecture sponsored by the Library School on the Florida State University campus, Edgar Dale called librarians' attention to the fact that printed books were not always respectably accepted in college libraries. During the fifteenth century, the Duke of Urbino "had a mind to do what no one had done for a thousand years or more; that is, to create the finest library since ancient times." But, adds Vespasiano Da Bisticci, the bookseller: "In this library all the books are superlatively good, and written with the pen, and had there been one printed volume it would have been ashamed in such company."[2]

Now, after all, Dr. Dale points out, are not these fearful, twentieth century librarians in danger of evaluating AV media in the same terms that their fifteenth century forerunner used to reflect on the products of the printing press? What is even more serious, asks Dr. Dale, are librarians not turning their backs on the real mission of libraries? The librarian, as Dr. Dale sees the problem, must not look upon himself ". . . merely as an agent for the custody and distribution of printed materials but also as an agency for the custody and distribution of illuminating ideas no matter whether they appear on tape, wax, film, paper, or a television screen."[3]

It is well to be recalled in this way to our professional mission. If we are dedicated to the dissemination of good ideas, first, then the format of these ideas must be of second importance. Our obligation becomes clear. As administrators of academic libraries we are responsible for the acquisition and dissemination of these ideas whether they appear in book, map, picture, recording, film, or any one of a dozen or more forms. As a matter of fact, it would be difficult indeed to discover a single academic library in these United States without some non-print materials.

For example, one chapter in any one of the standard AV textbooks deals with maps and globes.[4] The fact that a cartographic unit is part of any respectable AV service argues nothing for removal of all geographic representations from the academic library. Maps have always been an integral part of college and university collections, and even the most conservative university librarian would probably concede that he is already partly in the AV business.

In addition to cartographic and graphic media, however, AV concerns itself with what audiovisualists call museum objects and with local resources. Do not be misled. Both classes of AV are now and have long been an integral part of library collections and services. Our exhibit cases are full of both art and science specimens, some owned outright by the library and others borrowed from instructional departments on the campus for the purpose of cooperative display. And as for local resources which provide the media of communication for field trips and school journeys, libraries have been a far more important accessory in the past than has generally been recognized. Consider, for example, the variety of local indexes developed—not only by public libraries, but by academic libraries—to various cultural, social, educational, and other agencies, to industrial and commercial activities in the town and county, to the faculty researches, interests, specialties, and hobbies, and yes, even to the natural resources of the campus environment. Without these library operations the field trips of AV would be less meaningful.

And so we come to the more frightening categories of AV materials. To the audiovisualist the "flat picture" is a must among media. Do not let the word "flat" frighten you. Library vertical files are full of pictures. Among library reference books there are even a few indexes to these same pictures. Even the conservative librarian who does not keep a picture file must admit he is not representative and that a great number of his colleagues have been AV for a long time.

But what about phono-records, as the *Saturday Review* now calls them. It does not take a very old librarian to recall the Carnegie collections of fine recordings presented to scores of colleges in the United States. Many of the college browsing rooms still maintain record libraries of good music, drama, elocution, and language. Other libraries have cooperated with foreign language departments to promote speaking as well as reading and writing in a foreign tongue. And in a few instances research on the campus has been assisted by the library's recording and preserving men's dialects and animals' sounds. Perhaps here the conservative university librarian would agree that the academic librarian has been and of right should be AV.

This brings us to the film and projected materials. Certainly there is no argument about the microfilm now. To us, the machine we use with it is a reader; to the audiovisualist, it is possibly just another projector. At the very least, it puts both librarian and audiovisualist in the same camp on the question of another format—a film format for the dissemination of ideas. Probably the one medium on which the librarian might balk is the 16mm motion picture. But an increasing number of all kinds of libraries are renting these films for classroom use and for library study; in some instances, they are even purchasing them.

It can be seen, therefore, class by class, that AV media are no strangers to libraries. They are simply other formats for ideas. Basically, they lend themselves to the library processes of acquisition, preparation, interpretation, and dissemination. Physically and financially they confront librarianship with certain peculiar problems, but with problems no more peculiar than the various classes of media already professionalized in our library literature.

Let's examine some of these problems. In the first place, the academic library should look toward the centralization of responsibility for AV media on campus. This need not mean centralization of housing, but it certainly should mean centralized inventory. Along with central inventory, coordinated acquisition should be sought. The argument is the same as that for centralization of print material acquired by the institution of higher education through its library.

In the second place, as soon as possible, the academic library should provide personnel qualified to serve the campus in as many of the AV media as possible. To begin with, the smaller library may assign the best-qualified staff member on a part-time basis. As soon as possible, however, the library should plan to employ a librarian trained in the AV field. Increasingly our library schools are incorporating AV courses and units in the basic professional curriculum, equipping a new generation of librarians for AV service.

In the third place, the agencies and departments of instruction most audiovisually inclined should be enlisted in developing a plan for the campus.

On most campuses the school or department of education and the extension agency will be in the AV vanguard. But let not the traditional scholar take comfort in that. The colleges of arts and sciences are by far the heaviest users of these AV media: 1) 16mm film, 2) glass slides, 3) maps, 4) opaque objects. Departments in the general college, in the sciences, and in the fine arts, among others, should therefore be approached early in any plan to coordinate AV services for the campus. A very good beginning is the appointment of a representative faculty committee on AV services to plan with the librarian. This could be either a sub-committee of the library committee, or a separate committee.

In the very beginning about eight basic aspects of AV services as aids to campus instruction and research should come under the survey by the library and its AV committee. The *cartographic unit* in embryo will already be functioning in most academic libraries. In cooperation with the history and geography departments and with other heavy users, the available maps, globes, atlases, and geographic services on the campus will be canvassed. Augmented indexing and cataloging will be undertaken where necessary and additional accessions recommended to support the campus' total holdings, now inventoried in the library. If production of special or local maps is called for, it will probably be decided to do the work in the geography department or in the library.

Next the *graphics unit* will come up for consideration. Civilian institutions are still lagging behind in instructional use of various charts, graphs, demonstrations, and other graphics used in military instruction. The average library, however, produces considerable bulletin board material and reproduces through mimeograph, lithograph, or photostat both research and instructional materials that might be filed for future reference. This the library frequently does for its own graphics. But on the campus various other graphics are being produced that are either stored in some department office or destroyed, though their value is not necessarily limited to a single use. If the library could at least start a campus pool of instructional graphics organized for subject use, another valuable contribution to the dissemination of ideas might well be made. Whether the library should undertake production of graphics material for various departments of the campus will need particular study in cooperation with the fine and industrial arts departments.

The third inventory will involve *museum objects*. Many of these are already in the library. Others are in various art and science departments. If the campus has a museum, a huge collection will be there. It is important to emphasize that the campus library does not have to become a museum, even though the British Museum is one of the greatest libraries in the world. But the library has an obligation to disseminate ideas no matter what their format. And in keeping with that mission the library should endeavor without duplication to organize for bibliographic dissemination the museum objects that will make more effective the instruction and research carried on by the institution. In this connection and in relation to other classes of library materials, the library should have opaque projectors available for departmental and library use.

A fourth inventory of local resources will consist basically of a review of the *indexing, abstracting, and other bibliographic services* now part of the library. Any human and environmental resources available within a convenient radius but not readily known should be cataloged and disseminated to the part of the campus concerned. Certainly, faculty planning field trips and expeditions should be expected to utilize what the library can contribute.

A fifth canvass will involve *pictorial illustrations* of all kinds—separate, in books and periodicals, in the art department, and elsewhere on campus. There is nothing new here for libraries. Many remarkable collections can be found in libraries now. Libraries without such collections will find untapped sources among citizens, alumni, friends.

A sixth investigation will involve *recordings*, both disc and tape. Increasingly the library must build its collections to serve the many departments that now use sound in instruction and research. The creation of listening posts in the reading rooms as well as acoustically treated listening rooms deserves campus librarians' consideration. The listening post in the reading room may have as many as six sets of earphones, thus providing the language, or music, or speech student with an auditory accompaniment to his reading effort. Tapes of significant radio programs may be the most valuable of all books for particular instructional situations. This means that the library must include tape recorders in its equipment as well as playbacks for discs.

The seventh consideration is *films*, and this is the one the worried librarian looks upon as the AV problem. Microtexts and the readers needed with them are already an integral part of the academic library. But the 16mm motion picture is not. What is more, the investment required for even a small collection of films—to say nothing of the projector—is disproportionate to the budget of the average small college library. There are two solutions to this budget problem. Film renting from the state library of films or from out-of-state film libraries is within the range of most libraries. Cooperative buying with other college libraries and the organization of film circuits provide an opportunity for each participating library to disseminate many highly effective instructional films to the departments using them. It must also be remembered that many of the best films are free. The steadily rising quality of the sponsored film is making it an ever more effective medium for college instruction.

Finally, the place of *radio and television* in the library must be thoroughly considered. Libraries are already indexing and disseminating information about good programs. Some libraries tape them. But the real library opportunity is in shaping television programs yet to come. In this connection I cannot resist quoting Edgar Dale's remarks to librarians:

> I should like to propose a slogan for libraries that may suggest what they can do: "Your library has the best ideas in the world." Through television you will have an opportunity to show . . . just what your resources are . . . books, reference materials, encyclopedias . . . in short, television gives you a showcase in every television home in your community. You can display your wares in their living room.[5]

These are some of the audiovisual dimensions of an academic library. Despite the general terms in which they have been presented, these dimensions are not only academic but applied. In at least one case when the library school dean advises the university librarian to go AV, there is a tangible basis for the advice. On the campus of Florida State University there is a centralized AV service, administered by the Library School in cooperation with the University Library and the various schools and colleges on the campus. All eight of the aspects are represented. Various degrees of centralization have been accomplished. But the growing concept of unity of library media is an unquestioned asset to both instruction and research. By means of all of the formats the world's best ideas are increasingly permeating higher education.

FOOTNOTES

1. Georges Duhamel, *In Defense of Letters* (New York, Greystone Press, 1939), p. ix.
2. *The Vespasiano Memoirs* (Lives of Illustrious Men of the XVth Century), trans. by William George and Emily Waters (New York, Lincoln MacVeagh, 1926), pp. 102, 104.
3. Edgar Dale, "The Challenge of Audio-Visual Media," in *Challenges to Librarianship*, ed. by Louis Shores (Tallahassee, Florida State University, 1953), p. 101.
4. See, for example, W. A. Wittich and C. F. Schuller's *Audio-Visual Materials: Their Nature and Use* (New York, Harper, 1953).
5. Dale, "The Challenge of Audio-Visual Media," p. 104.

THE MEDIUM JUNIOR COLLEGE

Because the junior college deals with the widest range of individual differences found anywhere in higher education, classroom-centered teaching must be replaced by carrel-centered independent study in which the faculty's role becomes primarily one of matching individual differences in students with individual differences in media. Other predictions of things to come by 1999 read like pure fantasy in 1969.

Tonight is March 27. But I ask you to imagine that the year is 1999.

Few of us remember the Fourth Annual Conference held here 30 years ago. But all of us know how fantastic have been the happenings of these past three decades.

In July 1969, our Apollo 11 and Russia's Sputnik 13 were poised on their pads for a race to be first to land on the Moon. But before either could take off, a moonship landed on earth.

Blushingly, our scientists said, "So you were the flying saucers." But the moonmen graciously admitted equal disbelief about our Apollo 8, which moon people reported as having passed certain points ten times. And, the moon scientists added, for years we insisted there could be no life as we knew it anywhere else in the solar system.

In that year, the United States concluded the Vietnam War, in response to the demonstration, and delivered millions of South Vietnamese to the North's totalitarianism. Disorders in town and gown hastened the brief dictatorship which almost realized for the United States George Orwell's *1984*.

In 1969, our United States seemed determined to prove the historical cycle theories of Toynbee. By all the signs of the sixties we were repeating the course of the rise and fall of great nations in the past. It seemed inevitable that we would provide documentation for another Gibbon.

As you recall, there were two major party lines in 1969 (the Establishment and the Demonstration). The traditionalists were referred to as the Establishment. They were held responsible for poverty and prejudice at home; war in Southeast Asia. Washington was its headquarters, and the President of the United States its leader.

Opposing them were the Marchers and the Picketers. History now identifies them as the Demonstration. They opposed war abroad, but increasingly stirred violence at home. They exhibited problems, but considered solutions not their responsibility.

Pessimism permeated both the Establishment and the Demonstration. What was wrong with something excited them much more than what was right. They outdid each other in denouncing President Lyndon B. Johnson. In the very year when the Demonstration was supporting the Russian demand that the United Nations get out of the United States, the Establishment was displaying bumper signs on their automobiles that read, "Get the United States out of the United Nations."

Reprinted with permission from *Illinois Libraries*, 51:499-508 (June 1969).

Not only our politics, but our culture as well was supposed to be dual. Indeed, one of the most frequently quoted essays in the sophisticated circles of 1969 was the English scientist C. P. Snow's "Two Cultures."

As we look back, science and its method appear to have had a near-monopoly on man's thinking. Not only was research the only answer for the physical, biological, and social sciences, but no history could be written without it. Even more shocking, in perspective, was the complete abdication of art to science. Novelists like Truman Capote boasted of their research. Realism became basic in fiction, drama, and even poetry. Precise, sensory descriptions of physical processes were the ultimate goal of the artist's effort.

So it was that during one Broadway season, 21 successive plays were praised by critics for courage in exposing deviations. Theaters were packed by the "oh-so-liberated" to view perversions, addictions, abnormalities in human behavior. For example, a play with the title "You Know I Can't Hear You When the Water's Running" had a profound opening scene in which the hero is to appear stark naked, slowly approaching the audience, on stage. This was to provide something "super arty" called "the shock of recognition." The play ran to a packed theater for well over a year.

Another darling of the Broadway stage included a bit of adolescent adultery between two faculty couples on a college campus, with the irrelevant title, *Who's Afraid of Virginia Woolf?* And if you didn't see the relevance, you were ostracized from the intellectual groups of both the Establishment and the Demonstration. Indeed, relevance in a title in those days counted heavily against the author. There was a gloomy play staged over and over again by amateur groups with a title so senseless that even now I am uncertain of the word sequence, and the one that makes the most sense is "The Hot Can on the Tin Roof." If theater in the latter days of Greece and Rome was an index of decline, the United States certainly had its counterparts in the 1960s.

Nor was the fiction less indicative of a society's permissive decay. An adolescent classic with the title *Catcher in the Rye* could more critically have been retitled "Pitcher in the Corn." Its unheroic theme, applauded more enthusiastically by adults than by the teenagers about whom it was written, once received this curt comment from a young adult library patron:

Librarian: You should read this book!

Y.A.: Why?

Librarian: Don't you want to know what goes on in a *private* school?

Y.A.: No, I'm having too much fun in *Public* School 88.

And on the adult fiction scene, one critic offered the readers six cliff-hanging seductions in what he considered the greatest novel of the century. A novel without four-letter words was considered dishonest by the sophisticates and almost unpublishable by publishers in the gold rush. Eighteenth century writers who lived in squalid attic rooms and ate one meal a day had it easy compared to the mid-twentieth century novelist who had to wait three months for his fourth Cadillac because the manufacturer did not have it in the precise pink color; or the realist who felt constrained to spend no more than $20,000 on his cocktail party.

Although it may appear to us now, in 1999, that our Hippie parents considered the four-letter word the Symbol of Intellectual Freedom, there was a Harvard math professor who changed, as he declared, from "Ed Biz" to "Show Biz" to parody the censorship concern in a permissive society.

As we now study the video tapes of 1969 television entertainment, we must temper our contempt for the appreciations of the older generation. Remember that they, too, considered the generation that preceded them hypocritical, dishonest, and unfair. In 1969 there was incessant repetition (by the middle-aged demagogue courting dissident youth) of the platitude, "Your generation has inherited problems you did not create"—as if this was true of no other young generation in the history of the world. There is, however, no suggestion that the Hippie generation guarantees to hand down a problemless world to the next generation.

It is easy for us to be critical of both the Establishment and the Demonstration, from our perspective. But we must remember that this nation had experienced the two most devastating world wars of all times; social and technological revolutions unprecedented in the record of civilization. What we must ponder is the overwhelming pessimism and realism that accompanied war and revolution. The question we must ask is "why did neither the Establishment nor the Demonstration have the courage of optimism and romanticism?" What made everyone so pragmatic? Why did they glory in such cliches as the "grass roots" and "keeping your feet on the ground"? Could they not, with their demonstrations for freedom, see that a word they loved so much, "groovy," suggests a rut? How could they all, leaders and followers, repeat *ad nauseam*, their smug references to the two "explosions" of population and information, and the two "gaps" of generation and credibility? Was there no one to point out how overestimated these gaps and explosions were, relatively speaking?

No doubt about it, 1969 was one of the very low points in the history of the United States. Our national collapse seemed inevitable. Violence ruled our cities. Abroad, it was considered smart to take money from America and call Americans ugly. But even worse was the defeatism at home. Our college campuses, which should have been the centers of intellectual effort, became circuses of exhibitionism. In the name of intellectual freedom, a minority occupied academic buildings, interfered with the rights of those who chose to go to classes, and shouted down speakers who disagreed with them. But out of this very campus chaos came the first revival of the creative optimism that had made this nation unique in the history of peoples.

There had been an old Establishment tradition that higher education was for the elite. Right here in Illinois, there had been a leader of the theory of elitism—Robert Maynard Hutchins, for many years head of the University of Chicago. But also here in Illinois, at Joliet in 1902, the public junior college movement had begun. From the start it pledged its faith in universal higher education. Whereas universities and four-year liberal arts colleges self-righteously proclaimed that they were restricted to "superior" students, meaning those who could make high grades in their predatory disciplines, the junior college boldly announced an open-door policy. By 1970 there were more high school graduates enrolled as freshmen in junior colleges than in all other kinds of higher educational institutions. This was significant not only for education, but for society as a whole. Instead of marching, picketing, sit-downing, and exhibitioning, against unjust discrimination, the junior college courageously and intellectually demonstrated a solution in which democracy functioned supremely.

That was only the beginning of a peaceful revolution with far-reaching effects. Universal higher education introduced the widest range of individual differences in college population ever known before. The old learning mode of classroom lockstep and teacher lecture became impossible. Indeed, it was the persistence of this antiquated method of education which was basically responsible for student disaffection with the kind of college education they were getting. And it was thus that the independent study movement began.

At first this was reserved for the honors students, the elite who could be trusted to use their time properly. But college after college began to discover that independent study was even more advantageous to other students. Antioch College introduced its autonomous courses for *all* students. Florida Presbyterian College tried suspending all classes for a month in January, with startling results. Emory University instituted Wonderful Wednesday. On the quarter system, all students there had been required to take three five-hour courses, in which students attended classes every day for five days a week. In 1968 Emory tried suspending all classes one day a week—Wednesday—and the faculty and students took to it so enthusiastically, that it was extended. Oklahoma Christian, providing an exclusive workbench for each student, established the principle that faculty and students could agree on class meetings as infrequently as they deemed necessary.

But it remained for the junior college boldly to revolutionize the learning mode. The library-college idea had been advanced as early as 1934. The movement spread slowly at first, but picked up momentum beginning in the sixties. By 1970 it had a quarterly journal and an active organization, Library-College Associates, Inc., with headquarters at the University of Oklahoma. The junior college picked up the idea and added new dimensions to it.

Junior college leaders well understood the reason for the classroom teaching mode of the past. Because media were available in limited quantities, the teacher had to present information orally to groups of students in the form of lectures. As long as college was limited to the so-called upper 10 percent, the spread of individual differences was not too wide, and the lecturer could pitch his presentation on an average that did not miss too many of his students.

But as more and more students entered college, the range of individual differences became so wide that an average presentation tended to bore the gifted and discourage the disadvantaged. Furthermore, by 1970, media of all formats, not only hardcover print, but paperbacks, graphics, projections, transmissions, and computer assisted media, began to proliferate at such a pace that, for the first time in the history of education, individual differences in students could be matched by individual differences in media. Individualized, independent study emerged as the obvious learning mode.

There were many obstacles in 1970, however, to immediate replacement of classroom-centered teaching by carrel-centered learning. Most classroom teachers felt insecure in this new learning mode. Although they might feel they knew their subjects, and more shakily claim to know their students, they were unsophisticated in media. This was so largely because their teacher education insisted on teaching media very gingerly, and *incidentally*. Largely because of junior college insistence, teacher education agencies began to introduce *per se* media instruction. Long before students were taught media in relation to subjects, or methods, or educational psychology, they were introduced to the whole range of media formats, from textbook to television, from magazine to motion picture.

But the old classroom teachers were not the only obstacles. Those who worked with media were divided. Librarians had a term which was always anathema to me—something they called "non-book materials." But they could never define it, except by pointing to projectors or other equipment that they didn't want to maintain or operate. You could put them on the spot, however, by asking them to identify as audiovisual such media formats as maps and globes, pictures, and even phonograph records. And audiovisualists talked of print as something quite apart. It troubled them, however, when transparency overlays began to appear in hardcover books, and the librarians began to take over microprojections like film and fiche, and micro-opaques like 3 by 5 cards and 6 by 9 prints, and when they renamed projectors, readers.

Nor did this decisiveness end with the audiovisual-librarian schism. Soon the televisionists began to pull away from the audiovisualists and build their own empire. And then the computerized information scientists separated into their own organization. Nor did the separation stop there. CAI became a whole empire when the exponents of computer-assisted instruction decided their mission was more important than information retrieval. So it happened on some campuses that these two media groups separated expensively by purchasing two different and usually incompatible computers. On our campus, for example, the information retrievalists switched to CDC, while the computer instructionists went to the IBM 360. All of this separatism bewildered education administrators and classroom teachers. For example, there were dual media centers—a so-called audiovisual center, and a library. Classroom teachers would be confident as to where to go if the format wanted was a 16mm film or a hardcover book. A map or a globe, however, could be in either place. If you wanted a picture, you had to call it "flat" to get it in the AV center; and if you wanted museum objects you'd have to ask for them as "realia" in the AV center. When you ordered music for your classroom, you specified phono-records in the library, but discs in the AV center.

As early as 1946, Florida began to bring the audiovisualists and librarians together. Out of their joint efforts emerged the first materials center, forerunner of the later learning resource center. Florida became the first state in the union to establish certification for all media personnel. It wasn't easy. Librarians and audiovisualists continued to be wary of each other. But at long last most of them began to see that in unity there was strength. A tangible result was that the legislature one year earmarked a million dollars to be used by the school for instructional materials. Out of this came the first unified textbook, often referred to as the shotgun marriage of audiovisualists and librarians—my book, *Instructional Materials*. The 1969 joint standards of DAVI and AASL was the first official vindication by both groups.

Despite these obstacles, the junior colleges spearheaded the new learning mode—independent study in individualized carrels, supported by classroom meetings only when a group of students felt the need to come together. As early as 1965, Oklahoma Christian College provided an individual carrel for each student. It was a radical step then, resisted by administrators as too expensive and uneconomical, although much more classroom space remained unused for longer periods of time. It was resisted by some educational psychologists who employed the now discredited questionnaire techniques of establishing that students didn't like carrels. And there was considerable reluctance in the ranks of classroom teachers and media personnel. But independent study overcame.

As we look at our media-sophisticated junior college faculties today, we wonder how teachers and students tolerated their frustrations. Some very fine teaching is being accomplished by the subtle matching of individual differences in students with individual differences in media. But, above all, students are learning with greater excitement through individual discovery. Instead of having pre-digested information fed to them by the lecturer, like pablum, they are acquiring many more facts much more rapidly by reading, viewing, listening, and even tasting, smelling, at their own dial access workbenches, the 1999 version of the student carrel.

Inevitably, this revolution in the learning mode converted the junior college library into the modern media center. The most striking change appeared in the philosophy of evaluation and selection of media. Librarians had always practiced something called "book selection," which meant to them acquisition of hard-cover print, primarily. Two of the last and finest aids in the junior college field were published in 1968—one by Frank Bertalan, the other by Helen Wheeler. Both were quality bibliographic works, both omitted what was then called "nonbook materials." This was especially handicapping to junior college librarians, because audiovisualists were less bibliographically minded, and there were no selection aids for other formats comparable to those prepared by librarians for print.

Gradually, the unity concept for media began to take hold. In 1957, I had done an editorial for the *Saturday Review* that first projected the concept of the generic book as the sum total of man's communication possibilities. Under this concept a film was as much a book as a hardcover collection of printed pages; or as the earlier formats of handwritten parchment manuscripts or hand-chiseled cuneiform clay tablets. I had indeed quoted a fifteenth century monastery librarian who considered the manuscript format to be the only book, while the new machine-produced print was "non-book materials."

Until 1970, book selection meant, primarily, selection by subject. I had tried to describe a three-pronged approach to selection, which was absolutely prerequisite to the developing concept of independent study. Almost as important as subject selection, I had insisted, were level selection and format selection. Selection by level had been easier to sell than format selection. There was a ready-made administration classification in what was then called K-6, 7-12, and 13-14 (for the junior college level). Indeed, a few book selection aids, like the *Children's Catalog*, had even offered a finer level discrimination in its grade-by-grade lists of books.

The format classification idea was hardest to sell, despite the celebrity exhibitionism of Marshall McLuhan. Perhaps this 95-year-old man will be forgiven for his professional jealousy. Marshall McLuhan had served with him, briefly, on the ASCD Commission on Instructional Materials before he had attained celebrity stature. Despite all of the TV exhibitionism, McLuhan stated one concept of extreme importance: the format of a medium may affect its communicability. My envy stems from the fact that this was the point I was desperately trying to communicate to my fellow librarians and audiovisualists in my writings and speakings. But I simply did not communicate it in the rock and roll of that age, a beat that McLuhan captured. However, his underestimation of print, his overemphasis on technology, and his density on extrasensory perception have been exposed by our 1999 perspective.

Now we select media for our junior college media libraries from all three approaches: level, subject, format. But we are much more conscious of format. We no longer make up lists of print format separately, and add audiovisual lists later, as they did back in 1969. We intercalate print, graphic, projection, transmission, resource, and computer materials, as some Florida materials centers began doing crudely in their card catalogs as far back as 1947.

This approach to media evaluation and selection has resulted in junior college library innovations. The computer printout catalog and range of automated technical processes have been much refined over the exaggerated beginning three decades ago. We place less emphasis on hardware than they did, largely because technology and the scientific method on which it is based are steadily declining in the face of our startling discoveries in parapsychology. Indeed, our whole theory of learning has been disrupted by the marvels of telepathy, clairvoyance, precognition, and most recently, psychokinesis. Although we used to consider the computer fast, it is now approaching horse and buggy status in the face of the instantaneous telepathic communication we have within us, which only awaits individualized development. It is difficult for us to understand how scientists who prided themselves on open-mindedness could have failed to recognize such a breakthrough mind as that of the great Joseph Banks Rhine, of Duke University.

Perhaps the best way to understand 1969 is through the curricula of the time. There was a hierarchy of subjects. The natural sciences were at the top, with the physical sciences just a bit more respectable than the biological ones. Most of the humanities were given the respect that goes to old age. Philosophy resisted the sacred method of science, but the arts and literature steadily abdicated to the dominant culture. As for the social sciences, they outdid each other to mimic the natural sciences. Sociology and education, particularly, because they had remained on the other side of the railroad track for so long in the academic community, often went to ludicrous quantitative extremes in their investigations. But what the curriculum suffered from most was a passionate commitment to specialism. If you had lived on a college campus then, as I did for four decades before retirement, you would have been convinced that Genesis should have been rewritten in terms of chemistry, mathematics, economics, psychology, grammar, and the other subjects the academicians had established as prime.

The junior college had a hard time. It had to begin by establishing three programs they called college parallel, terminal, and continuing. And these two-year upstarts had to swear on the Bible that never would these three programs be permitted to mix. Once a student was cast as a terminal, he had to keep his place, and get no uppity ideas about college parallel.

The junior college changed this curriculum artificially—and not too soon. For the United States was suffering from a shortage of carpenter, plumber, electrician, and other manual talents. It took the junior college to restore the whole man, and the whole woman, perspective. The junior college, while insisting that every citizen had a manual obligation to his community, nevertheless recognized that the quality of citizenship was improved when everyone was exposed to the concepts and abstractions of higher education.

As a result, the junior college contributed a new curriculum perspective. Led by library media generalists, it introduced the knowledge overview at the beginning and the knowledge capstone systhesis at the end. These two courses, as you know, have become common requirements: the specialisms elective.

To reinforce the independent study learning mode, the junior college, again led by its generalists, introduced an augmented course on media, required of all students. If half of knowledge is knowing where to find it, then the time had come to give some earnest attention to this half.

Finally, as a contribution to what 1969 liked to call the "generation gap"—an exaggeration even in 1969, when the gaps were greater within the generations than between them—the junior college introduced the idea that the curriculum should not be limited to what is significant to the older generation, but should also consist of what is significant to the younger generation. Thus again, the media generalist showed the junior college the way, by introducing the student interest profile. After the faculty indicated, through syllabi, the curriculum content considered significant by the older generation, students were invited to indicate in ranked order their deepest interests and greatest involvements, no matter how inconsequential their elders might consider these. Student profiles are weighted as heavily as faculty choices in media selection.

Well, there we are in 1999 with another revolting younger generation. Those of us who wore beards in 1969, glorified in our love-ins, denounced the older generation as squares, liked to hear our elders sympathize with us for inheriting problems we didn't create, and were ready to march at the drop of a hat, now find it hard to tolerate the dissent of our own youth. We can't understand why they shave their heads; call music with a beat corny; like romanticism with happy endings; roar with laughter over realism; refuse to believe that their parents could have lined up for any movie as dull as *Bonnie and Clyde*. Perhaps they are nearer the truth than we. I seem to recall that there was a musical in our time called *Man of La Mancha* in which Don Quixote said, "It takes less courage to describe things as they are, than as they should be."

PART IV:

MEDIA EDUCATION

THE MEDIUM WAY

Independent study has become an inevitable trend in current education experimentation and innovation. Because the key to independent study is media sophistication, all of us who work with media—librarians, audiovisualists, information scientists—have suddenly been thrust into leading roles in the education drama.

American education has a new learning mode. In two words, it can be identified as independent study, with the next most important word being "library." Winslow Hatch pointed out, not long ago, that one measure of quality in education was "the degree to which students can study independently."[1]

In the new learning mode, the student has his own individual workbench, called a carrel. Here he works with the generic book, in all of its varied formats, under the direction of a bibliographically sophisticated faculty. In higher education the ultimate form of this mode is the library-college. In grades "K-12" we find emerging something I have called the "medium school."

The trend to independent study is a concomitant of the national commitment to universal education. As more students enter our schools and colleges, the educational challenge of quantity is second only to the educational challenge of quality. We are now confronted by the widest range of individual differences ever. The classroom teaching mode is no longer able to cope with the spread of talents that meets as a group for cramped exercises of recitation and note-taking. At long last, we are being convinced that something must be done about individual differences. And the answer is independent study, tailored to the talents of the individual student.

As librarians, we can no longer avoid the implications of this independent study trend. For years we have celebrated our support of the classroom. But if the classroom is soon to become secondary to the carrel, what then will we support? Will we continue our role of supplier? Will we continue to acquire, process, and circulate the materials of instruction as we have done in the past, making an occasional feint at learning through something we have called "reference" or, more recently, "information science"? Or will we accept the challenge hurled at us by Chancellor Branscomb in his classic study for the Carnegie Corporation, published under the hardcover title *Teaching with Books*? He wrote in 1940, as some of us will recall: "To sum up, it may be said without hesitation that the fundamental need of the college library is to develop a distinctive program of its own."[2]

Now is the time for libraries in the schools, as well as in the colleges, to develop a distinctive educational program of their own. National commitment to universal education, the widening range of individual differences, student revolt against the classroom lockstep, and an inept grouping by faculty

Reprinted with permission from the *Kentucky Library Association Bulletin*, 32:14-21 (January 1968).

colleagues, who are less qualified to exploit the mushrooming independent study movement, cry out for our help. The situation demands a new dimensional approach by librarianship. More than ever before, our profession must abandon its ancillary complex, its supportive role, and its devotion to management and housekeeping; our profession must assume educational leadership.

The reason is simple. For the first time in the history of education, instructional materials are so many and so varied that individual differences in students can be matched with individual differences in media. These media make independent study feasible; they also render the classroom mode uneconomical and ineffective as a primary educational method.

But media learning requires a new breed of faculty. It requires teachers who know not only their students but their media. Despite Dr. Branscomb's expose of college faculty ineptness in teaching with books, we all know many classroom teachers in schools, as well as in colleges, who are library-minded. But we know, also, that there are many more librarians who know books and libraries than there are classroom teachers. So, to begin with, we librarians are in a better position than any of our educational colleagues to teach in this new learning mode called independent study. The only question is, how many of us are willing to *library teach* rather than to *library manage*?

Before we answer this question, let's dispose of the pragmatic one—the one we like to call the "grass roots" or "feet on the ground" question. Who will acquire and accession; classify and catalog; circulate; collect fines on overdues; read and revise shelves; check periodicals, documents, continuations? And on and on. I agree that these questions must be answered. I want a neat, efficient, quiet, well-organized library as much as anyone. But I do not want it at the expense of the high educational role we have long denied our profession.

My answer to these practical questions on library keeping is appearing in current library management trends. Two of the most important trends are to machines and to technicians. Our mechanical heritage has made us more susceptible to the dramatics of automation than to the prosaics of semi-professionals. With frenzy, we often buy and install hardware first, and justify it later. Not so long ago, I visited a library with printout catalog, computerized serial records, systems studies galore, and serious consideration of LDX (long distance Xeroxing) with remote consoles already under demonstration. I asked, "How is the innovating going?"

"Confidentially," she whispered, "it takes longer and it costs more, but we've doubled our library budget, and the President escorts more visitors, personally, to the library than he ever did before."

Of course, there has been much unnecessary automation. But most of the hardware has relieved professional librarianship of the routine that has contributed unfavorably to our professional portrait. For instance, I believe the printout book catalog will inevitably replace our 3 by 5 files. This will eliminate much of the routine processing that professional personnel dissipate their efforts on, and will free us for creative literature searching and bibliographic description. Through offset printers, we will be able to furnish selected indexes to any part of the collection by subject, level, format, and in the preferred relations desired by a specialist for his immediate purpose. The only remorse I see about this aspect of computerized technical processing is on the part of those of us who have committed millions of dollars to reclassifying by LC, when we at last understand that a simple ID number is easier for the computer, and that any broad classification for the physical book, such as the Dewey Third Summary, is adequate.

We have been somewhat less receptive to the idea of a technician level of semi-professional competence, although the present high ratio of professionals to clericals in our library staffs should concern us. Some of us are concerned with another library education articulation problem caused by the proposed junior college technician program. After many years of resistance, we have finally correlated the NCATE undergraduate and ALA graduate programs. But some of us in library education do not yet see the correlative opportunity in the junior college program—a way to relegate many of the techniques that keep our courses from gaining full graduate and senior division respectability.

And some of us in library practice fear that many of the techniques we have enjoyed in the past will be taken from us by a whole new class of semiprofessionals. It is disadvantageous both to the library and to professional librarianship to continue to spend so much time on these necessary but semiprofessional tasks. Nor does such devotion enhance the professional image we hope to use in recruitment. Within recent months, some of our most promising graduates have written of disenchantment with library practice because of the disproportionate time required for routines that could more effectively be performed by technicians. Despite the New York State conclusion[3] of several years ago (and to me the conclusions did not seem to follow the findings), there has been a solid movement for a junior college technician program, and at least one state plans to launch such a program in its community junior colleges.[4]

Assuming that machines and technicians will inevitably relieve the professional librarian of many, if not most, of the techniques we have undertaken in the past, what will he do now? For one thing, he will become a full partner in research. He will not only retrieve information for the scientist, but will interpret it as well. What is more, he will carry on a part of the investigation, and in some instances make the discovery, or come up with the invention that will deserve the Nobel Prize. But research and the future of librarianship belong to another essay.

For another thing, the librarian will become a full partner in education. He will not only support the classroom, if there still is a classroom, but will provide an even more effective learning locus in the library carrel. No longer will the librarian slavishly follow a course of study constructed by others. Instead, he will be in the vanguard of curriculum development, presenting colleges and schools for the first time with a phenomenon of content following the library, rather than *vice versa*. From my comparative education and experience in librarianship's book selection, and pedagogy's curriculum development, I'd rather trust the education of the next generation to the former than to the latter.

Let me particularize on two major aspects of our professional role in the new learning mode of independent study. Without knowledge of books and libraries there can be no independent study. If the Monteith experiment[5] proved anything, it is that the library sophistication of both faculty and students is inadequate for the independence required by the new learning mode. Consequently, one of our highest and most creative commitments must be to educate the next generation of teachers and students to a sophisticated library use far beyond anything that has yet resulted from our orientation periods or even from our separate freshman courses.

To accomplish a new dimensional, library-use instruction, we will first have to be sure we are ourselves adequately reoriented. I approve of the new variations on the term "library" (like "learning resources center," etc.) only as a dramatic label to capture financial support from school boards and college presidents who have not been too bookish themselves in the past.

Before you shake your head and insist that a learning resource center is something different from a library, let me remind you that Florida pioneered the instructional materials concept and the materials center, forerunner of the current learning resource center name. The Library School of Florida State University was the first ALA-accredited graduate school to require audio-visual competence of all of its graduates. The literature will attest to my own personal crusade for the unity of materials concept, dating back to the first audiovisual course ever offered in the South, back at Peabody in 1935. My book, *Instructional Materials*, was probably the first textbook for teachers to treat the whole range of educational media, from textbook through television.[6]

What I must insist on at the outset is that we reorient ourselves to consider all formats in the whole range of instructional materials as part of the generic book. In our professional vocabulary, henceforth, the term "non-book materials" must be banished, as it has been for some time among Florida instructional materials specialists. In our concept, the film must become a book as much as the hardcover volume is. We must see our reluctance with audiovisual media in historical perspective with the fifteenth century librarian of a monastery collection, who declared shortly after Gutenberg's first imprint: "This is a true library. Here one will find only hand-written manuscripts, and not any of those machine-made reproductions that some have the audacity to call books."

The generic book concept has a basic educational idea that Marshall McLuhan, in my opinion, has only partially exploited. The educational idea may be simply stated in this way: if learning is fundamentally communication between learner and environment, then the format of the medium of communication may influence learning. In the past, our library classifications have considered subject the all-important approach to knowledge. More recently, level of difficulty, measured essentially by vocabulary, has been an important consideration. Now, for the first time, we have begun to realize—largely, probably, as a result of McLuhan's spectaculars—that medium format may be as important as subject or level in a particular learning situation.

Many examples from my teaching experiences, and yours, could be drawn to illustrate the superiority of film, or transparency, or tape or field trip, or globe, or, yes, hardcover print, for a particular subject at the mental age of the individual student concerned. Botany teachers who have used time-lapse photography know how much more effectively this kind of 16mm motion picture communicates plant growth than almost any other medium format. And what can compare with the tape of Latin American children's voices in homey conversation for communicating the nuances of pronunciation that Spanish teachers often desperately try to convey through print. But don't sell print as short as McLuhan does. The hardcover, the magazine, the government document can still communicate messages that all of the other formats together could not do. And as for factfinding, there are certain system designs in our basic reference books that our information science colleagues might well study in their retrieval efforts.

So we separatist audiovisualists, information scientists, and librarians must, first of all, reorient ourselves in the generic book. Those of us who believe the film, or the flat picture, or the tape, or the peep box does everything, need to rediscover the power of print. And the information scientist who believes passionately that the system is the thing, might well spend a few hours away from key punch and computer reexamining encyclopedists' struggles with information retrieval. But above all, the librarian with my mechanical ineptness needs to disillusion himself that audiovisual means electronic specialism, or even the annoyance of replacing a burnt-out bulb. What audiovisual really means is an extension of the means of communication between learner and his environment; and the librarian must make himself as knowledgeable in these other formats of the generic book as he now is in the formats we lump under the heading of print.

Once we have this reorientation ourselves, the first element in our new professional role as librarian, audiovisualist, information scientist, or media specialist is to sophisticate the next generation in the use of the tools for independent study. We must do this in a more imaginative way than we have taught the use of libraries and instructional materials in the past. Dramatically, we must present the whole repertoire of formats, generally at first, and then by subject and level. We must somehow convince teacher education that it is as important to teach media *per se* as it is to teach them incidentally to subject, to level, to method, and to what not. So a major part of our professional attention shifts from management to teaching—teaching the tools of independent study to a new generation of students and to a new breed of teachers.

The second major aspect of our new educational role is to introduce a new *gestalt* into curriculum development. Since World War II, at least, we have had a concurrent though comparatively mild effort to balance our rage for specialism with some generalism. The colleges call it general education. In the curriculum it has resulted in the substitution of an integrated course of "physical science" for such specialized beginning courses as chemistry, physics, or geology; and of a general course called "humanities" for literature, art, music, and philosophy. Although the movement had to struggle, at first, against the specialists, it has finally become accepted in many, if not most, institutions of higher education.

The time has come for the next step in *gestalt*. C. P. Snow called our attention to the schism between the two cultures of science and humanities. I agree with him that the schism exists, but I disagree with his opinion that the scientists are more aware of the humanities than the humanists are of the sciences. However that may be, I am in agreement that the time has come for a general course, or division, in our curriculum that cuts across the science and the humanities, and draws the social sciences and all of the applications into an overview of knowledge.

From the nature of our pedagogues' and specialists' curriculum, you would gather that the account in Genesis should be corrected to read, "On the first day, God was a chemist and created the elements; on the second day, He was an economist and created the means of production, consumption, distribution, at least, if not of exchange; and on the third day, He was a musicologist and created the sounds of the spheres; etc." Certainly, the student who moves from a chemistry class to a class in economics, to a class in art appreciation has such an order of creation confirmed for him every Monday, Wednesday, and Friday of each week during the academic year. The time has come to show God's universe as a whole, for the unity it unquestionably is. And no one can do this better than the faculty who work with the generic book.

The librarian or the media specialist is naturally a generalist. From time immemorial he has maintained his neutrality among the disciplines, serving them all impartially. Furthermore, through his classification of knowledge, the librarian has done much with the class called "generalia." He has had a major influence on the encyclopedia, the medium which is concerned with presenting a summary of the knowledge most significant to mankind. By the nature of his competence, the librarian is equipped to enter the curriculum with the most significant area of all, which, for want of a better distinguishing course title, we may simply call "knowledge." As I see it, every curriculum from "K through 14" (since junior college is basically general education) should have an overview at the beginning, and a capstone at the end. These would give relationship and perspective to the hallowed and predatory courses, subjects, disciplines, that we have for so long celebrated academically.

Not only does the librarian have the content for such an area from his practice in general book selection, but he has also a method, the forerunner of independent study, which we call professionally by such terms as browsing, reader advisory, or book listing. These professional methods of ours are the very heart of teaching in the independent study learning mode.

Innovation is affecting this nation's entire gigantic education effort. At the center of experimentation is the trend to independence in learning. Some one hundred colleges, like Antioch and Stephens, Elmira and Florida Presbyterian, Oklahoma Christian and Jamestown, are in the vanguard of the development now known as the library-college, a college which is completely a library, and in which the carrel has replaced the classroom as the center of learning. Uncounted high school systems, like Ridgewood, Illinois, and numerous elementary schools, like those of Shaker Heights, Ohio, are trying to see how far pupils can study independently under teacher guidance. The librarian or media specialist must, of course, continue to support the classroom teachers who carry on conventionally. We have a special responsibility to those classroom teachers who are working with students at all levels of competence to develop independence of the classroom. But above all, we owe ourselves a try at our own brand of education. We must accept Chancellor Branscomb's challenge, and see if we can come up with a solution of our own, for the most daring educational undertaking the history of the world has ever known—the higher education of all of the people.

Because I believe ours is a profession of destiny, I have faith that we will develop this new learning mode for the better education of the next generation.

FOOTNOTES

1. Winslow Hatch, *New Dimensions in Higher Education* (Washington, U.S. Office of Education, 1966).

2. Harvie Branscomb, *Teaching with Books* (Chicago, Association of American Colleges, 1940).

3. New York (State) University. Commissioner of Education's Committee to Evaluate the Experimental Library Technician Program, *Report* (Albany, N.Y., 1961).

4. Louis Shores, "Junior College Technician Program," *California Libraries*, 1967.

5. Patricia Knapp, *The Monteith College Library Experiment* (Metuchen, N.J., Scarecrow Press, 1966).

6. Shores, *Instructional Materials* (New York, Ronald Press, 1966).

DESIGN FOR TEACHER EDUCATION
IN INSTRUCTIONAL MATERIALS

The education of the media specialist for our schools was designed at least 13 years before DAVI and AASL gave joint consideration to this need. Well ahead of the rest of the nation, Florida certification was the realization of this concept. Several teacher education agencies—notably Southern Illinois University, Purdue, San Jose State, and St. Cloud (Minnesota)—pointed the way. Substitute the term "media" for "instructional materials" and you can appreciate how much the Florida design anticipated the national trend.

This could take the form of an open letter to the deans of schools of education and the heads of departments in teacher education institutions:

You now have among your offerings some or all of these courses: 1) children's literature; 2) library science; 3) audiovisual. You know there is a relationship among them. Increasingly your schools are asking you to give all teachers some instruction in these areas. What is more, the Index of Teacher Demand[1] tells you that the ratio of demand to supply in library science is now the highest of that in any teaching field—even higher than elementary education. You can't escape your responsibility. What can you do?

CERTIFICATION IN THE AREA OF INSTRUCTIONAL MATERIALS

Well, first off you can look at certification requirements and trends. About 40 states and the District of Columbia certify school librarians.[2] Four of these states also certify audiovisualists. Furthermore, most of the states indicate that all elementary teachers should be prepared in the area of children's literature, audiovisual aids, or library materials as teaching tools. Many of the states make comparable recommendations for secondary teachers.

Discernible in all of these recommendations is a trend toward unity. Overwhelmingly, educational leaders do not want to increase the number of special certifications. Separate certifications for audiovisual means two certifications in instructional materials instead of one. Dual certification encourages two resource centers instead of one in each school. This increases costs, complicates administration, and confuses the ultimate consumers—the teachers and pupils. Among school materials there is no clear line that divides audiovisual from other instructional materials. The desire of most administrators, therefore, is for a single certification in the area of instructional materials.

EDUCATION IN THE AREA OF INSTRUCTIONAL MATERIALS

To match this interest in a single certification, teacher education agencies are seeking a design for one program in instructional materials that

Reprinted with permission from the *Peabody Journal of Education*, 34:66-70 (September 1956).

will bring together courses in children's literature, library science, and audiovisual. At the moment, teacher education institutions are confronted by the specifications of three accreditation programs. The first of these is the master's program for librarianship accredited by the American Library Association.[3] Last year the NEA Department of Audio-Visual Instruction approved a master's program in audiovisual education.[4] In cooperation with the AACTE, the American Library Association also developed an undergraduate program for school librarians.[5] Various state and regional accreditation agencies are reviewing their instructional materials patterns and relating them to certification revision.

Looking at all of these efforts it is apparent that any design for teacher education in the area of instructional materials must adopt certain principles:

1. Every classroom needs a teacher who can select and utilize all kinds of instructional materials, suitable for his grade level and subject areas.

2. Every school building needs at least one teacher who can select, organize, administer all kinds of materials, and who can help teachers and pupils utilize these materials more effectively.

3. Every school system (county or city) needs a supervisor to direct the overall instructional materials program for all of the schools, administer a central clearinghouse for the dissemination of information, and maintain central processing for the procurement and cataloging of materials and equipment.

4. The education of these three classes of educational personnel should be articulated with each other and with teacher, library, and audiovisual education.

5. All classes of school materials should be represented, with no attempt to separate "audiovisual" from "library materials" since they are usually the same.

THE OVERALL DESIGN

Instructional materials should fit into the pattern of teacher education as a whole. Considering 124 semester hours the average quantitative requirement for the bachelor's degree, the distribution is approximately as follows:

1. General education, 45 semester hours
2. General professional teacher education, 20 semester hours
3. One academic or teacher major, 24 semester hours
4. Free electives, 35 semester hours

The instructional materials courses listed in the table below should fit easily into this distribution for classroom teachers and building librarians or coordinators.

The system supervisor should have at least five years of school experience and a master's degree that will include (beyond the basic 21 semester hours) courses in curriculum supervision, administration, and specialization in one class of instructional materials—such as children's books, educational television, motion pictures—or in one aspect of the instructional materials program, such as reference services or classification and cataloging.

THE PROGRAM (BACHELOR'S DEGREE)

X = Required

Sequence Course Title	Sem. Hrs.	Elem. Tchrs.	Sec. Tchrs.	Bldg. Lbns.	System Supervisors
1. Introduction to Instructional Materials (Grades 1-6)	3	X		X	X
2. Introduction to Instructional Materials (Grades 7-12)	3		X	X	X
3. Organization and Administration of a School Materials Center	3			X	X
4. Principles of an Instructional Materials Program	3			X	X
5. Reference Materials and Methods	3			X	X
6. Classification and Cataloging of Materials	3			X	X
7. Preparation and Production of Materials	3			X	X

THE COURSES

The seven basic courses in instructional materials should include two overviews in selection and utilization of all kinds of instructional materials. One of these overviews should concern itself with instructional materials suitable for grades 1-6; the other for grades 7-12. The first course should be required of all elementary classroom teachers; the second of all secondary classroom teachers; and both should be required of all building librarians and system supervisors.

The next five courses should be required only of building librarians and system supervisors. Course three, following the first two courses, should concern itself with the organization and administration of a school materials center. Included would be such matters as procurement of materials and equipment, prices, discounts, jobbers; organization of the materials for use; booking and charging systems; housing and equipment; budgets and finance; utilization devices.

Course four is the philosophy and principles course concerned with the concepts of an instructional materials program. It would trace the evolution of teaching materials, the impact of the two waves of the multi-materials method of teaching—library and audiovisual—on the school program, and the thinking of educational leaders from Horace Mann to the present on the role of instructional materials in the nation's schools. Other topics would deal with professional organizations, publications in the field, and ethics relating to selection and censorship.

Course five is a utilization course with emphasis on sources of information and ways to find out. If, as has often been quoted, "half of knowledge is knowing where to find it," this course deals with that half. Use of dictionaries, encyclopedias, atlases, maps, globes, indexes, bibliographies, and guides to films, filmstrips, recordings and other materials contributes to the making of a rich course.

The sixth course details the subject that too many consider the essence of librarianship. Classification and cataloging of instructional materials are fundamental to adequate use and considerable attention should be given to this subject. It is doubtful, however, that each school should do its own classification and cataloging. The trend is certainly in the direction of central classification and cataloging for all of the schools at the system level. Nevertheless, each librarian needs to know enough about the subject to assist fellow teachers in adequate utilization.

The seventh basic course is a laboratory course in the production of all kinds of school materials. It will include bulletin board, exhibit, poster, and display preparations. It may include training in the use of such equipment as dry and wet mounts, and the production of glass slides, film strips, and transparencies for the overhead projector, mimeograph and multigraph material, tapes, and color photos. There may be units on radio and television production and even some simple background in motion picture techniques.

These seven basic courses will at once be seen to comprehend the content of the present isolated and separate courses in children's literature, library science, and audiovisual. But it is quite evident also that these courses do much more. They relate the various formats of school materials to each other and to the objectives of the school. Out of such an articulated program, inevitably, a new generation of classroom teachers will be born—teachers inspired by the potential of a variety of instructional media for helping meet the problems of individual differences in children.

A GENERATION OF MEDIA TEACHERS:
The Curriculum Library's Role in Teacher Education

Curriculum libraries, laboratories, and materials centers emerged as new forces in teacher education, both in-service (in state and county school systems) and pre-service (in teacher education agencies). Some new dimensions spearheaded by the media movement and the trend to independent study are suggested here.

This generation of teachers faces a new relationship to pupils in the learning process. Of all the trends in American education, none is more challenging than that of independent study. If it continues, both learners and teachers will need a bibliographic competence that neither has ever had before, for the essence of independent study is matching individual differences in students with individual differences in materials. To accomplish this, and to achieve our national goal of universal education, we will need a new generation of media teachers. Our curriculum laboratories should be dedicated to the bibliographic education of those who teach.

Before I am accused of loose terminology, let me say that if I have to choose between a curriculum library and a curriculum laboratory, the latter is more suited to my thesis. I agree most earnestly with Robert E. Browne of the California State Department of Education that

> a library does not become a laboratory by placing the name "laboratory" on the door of a facility designed exclusively for the collection, housing and circulation of educational literature. Unless workshop activities involving the creative use of the publications are an integral part of the operation, the term "laboratory" is obviously a misnomer.[1]

The type of facility I am concerned with, and have been responsible for since 1946 at Florida State University, does collect, house, organize, and circulate a variety of materials. But it does much more. I hope its use of the materials will be considered extraordinarily creative. Incidentally, we have complicated terminology further by using neither term. We are a "materials center," with a unique dual obligation to two professional schools on the campus: the School of Education and the Graduate Library School. In the early days, we called ourselves LSMFT—that is, Library Science and Materials for Teachers.

Before I began the activation of a new library school at Florida State University in 1946, I had spent the decade preceding World War II on the Peabody campus, directing another library school. One of my most stimulating faculty colleagues there was Henry Harap, frequently considered the father of the curriculum laboratory idea. He arrived at Peabody in 1937, and since by that time I was already a veteran on the campus, I exchanged my background in Peabody and in library science with his ideas on a curriculum laboratory for the division of surveys and field services. In that division, by

Based on an address before the County and Curriculum Librarians Section of the California School Librarians' Association, San Francisco, March 4, 1966.

the way, curriculum history was made. A Rockefeller grant had set it up. Frank P. Bachman was its first director; Doak S. Campbell its second, later in association with Hollis Caswell. These two authored the curriculum development book that served as the Bible in the field for a decade. When Henry Harap joined the division, he went to work almost immediately on the laboratory.

Henry had the natural talents we most frequently associate with the stereotype image of the librarian. He was systematic, almost to the point of becoming a campus legend. Dr. Ed Wight (of the University of California, Berkeley) will confirm that their morning tennis match was played precisely from 7:18 to 7:48 a.m., because Henry's work day began at 8:00, and he had precisely timed the distance from tennis court to office. We recall that his third child was delivered by his wife in the hospital before 7:00 a.m., and several of us heard him express his appreciation for this timing, because it permitted him to begin his working day on schedule.

I watched Henry collect and organize a pioneer curriculum library. That it also became a laboratory there can be no doubt, in view of the Peabody contribution to professional literature. From him I learned something of the nature of the materials to be collected by a curriculum laboratory. Although his organization of these materials varied somewhat from the principles that I had been taught at Columbia, and that I was then teaching at Peabody Library School, there was so much homemade ingenuity in his organizational decisions that I rethought many of my filing-indexing theories.

Even more important than the kinds of materials and the way to organize them, however, I got from Henry Harap an idea of the real need for the curriculum laboratory. The immediate purpose was to provide the resources for curriculum study, improvement, and development. On campus I saw teaching and learning, not only in enriched curriculum courses, but in education courses in general, and in science, social science, language arts, and physical education.

Off campus, the division had begun its series of consultantships in state curriculum development. I recall participating in the Virginia project with the late Ullin Leavell, and in efforts with several of the other states. My librarian soul revolted often at the ancillary position of bibliography in the whole process of curriculum development. Sometimes it was as bad as this: "Here is a course of study we have constructed for this local school system. Louis, will you now compile a bibliography to go with it?" It reminded me of the time when the principal of our own demonstration school protested. We had a university librarian who spoke, wrote, and preached that librarians of teachers' colleges and secondary schools must study pedagogy, must know more about professional education. I could not have subscribed to anything more wholeheartedly. Part of his sermon was that the library must follow the curriculum. Day after day the librarian lectured the principal on this. The principal came to me in desperation one day to ask for $1.75 from the library school budget to buy some catalog cards for his school librarian. "Every time my school librarian asks the university librarian, who is her boss, for supply money, he insists she and I must study our curriculum first, so the library can follow it. I declare," he said, "when I walk down the hall I have the uncomfortable feeling that something uncanny, the curriculum, is following me."

I wanted to say to that university librarian what I have so often wanted to say to school librarians who had just become aware of professional education: not only should the library follow the curriculum, but perhaps the curriculum should follow the library. Not only does the librarian need to know something about professional education, but the teacher, supervisor and administrator need to know something about professional librarianship. Out of this Peabody experience grew the conviction that every curriculum library should be a curriculum laboratory—a creative, active force for building a better generation of teachers. Out of this experience came the idea for the Materials Center we activated at Florida State University concurrently with the activation of the Library School.

In the summer of 1947, our School of Education initiated the first of a series of annual educational leadership conferences, and invited the Library School to share in the effort. Partly because of these leadership conferences, and partly because the Dean of the School of Education had asked the Dean of the Library School to develop a curriculum library for them, it was decided to augment the usual library school laboratory library for the training of librarians with a curriculum library for the training of teachers. Recognizing from the start that the accents in a campus curriculum library frequently vary from those found in school system curriculum libraries, it was also decided to provide a model that our 67 Florida county school systems might follow.

Two other factors influenced our Materials Center version of a curriculum laboratory. One of these was the request that we also serve the State Department of Education, located about a mile from the campus, which had no materials laboratory of its own. The other was my determination that audiovisual media, which I had introduced for the first time at Peabody in 1935, should be an integral part of every librarian's and teacher's professional education. In 1947 we invited Amo DeBernardis of Portland, Oregon, to be our visiting consultant in audiovisual education. Subsequently, we added to our faculty Charles Hoban as audiovisual professor, and we invited such visiting consultants as Edgar Dale, Paul Witt, and Charles Schuller.

The figure below indicates, in terms of an adaptation of the format classification I developed for my book *Instructional Materials*,[2] the principal content categories for a curriculum materials center. Included, of course, are most of the classes of materials found in curriculum libraries and laboratories. For example, McVean[3] in his frequency of use ranking of curriculum laboratory categories of materials, placed textbooks first, followed by courses of study, units of work, lesson plans, and then standardized tests.

MEDIA FORMATS:
Content Categories for a Materials Center (Curriculum Laboratory-Library)

A. PRINT
    1. Textbooks: adoptions, non-adoptions; historical; workbooks
    2. Courses of study: local, state
    3. Reference books: dictionaries, encyclopedias, etc.
    4. Ephemera: pamphlets; clippings; publishers' blurbs
    5. Periodicals: professional education; library; audiovisual

    6. Teaching aids: manuals; lesson plans; units of work
    7. Tests: standardized; local
    8. Children's books: easy, imaginative, subject; young adult
    9. Evaluation: reports on Florida schools; other
   10. Professional books: education; library science; audiovisual instruction; educational psychology

B. GRAPHICS
    1. Pictures: flat, stereo photos; drawings
    2. Exhibits: chalk, bulletin, flannel, peg, magnetic boards; materials; dioramas, murals, posters
    3. Charts: graphs, diagrams
    4. Maps: globes; terrestrial and celestial
    5. Objects: specimens, models, mockups

C. PROJECTIONS
    1. Opaque: graphics
    2. Transparent: slides, filmstrips, films, transparencies
    3. Micro: texts and repros

D. TRANSMISSIONS
    1. Discs: monaural, binaural; music, language, sounds
    2. Tapes: monaural, binaural; music, language, sounds
    3. Radio: schedules; transcriptions
    4. TV: schedules; kinescopes; video tapes

E. COMMUNITY RESOURCES
    1. Natural: target folders, field trip reports; publications
    2. Social; directory; target folders; field trip reports; publications
    3. Persons: directory; tapes; visuals; clippings

F. MACHINE
    1. Teaching machines: devices; programmed materials
    2. Computer: printouts; programs

All of these classes of materials are used heavily by faculty and students in our Materials Center. But because of our special accents, some other categories have almost equal use. For example, our very good collection of children's books is used as constantly by School of Education students as by Library School students, because all elementary education majors are required to take the Library School course to meet certification requirements.

The Library School activated an audiovisual center and audiovisual courses in 1947. As a consequence, films, filmstrips, tapes, discs, slides, transparencies, and the whole gamut of what are called audiovisual materials constitute a heavily used category. Our Materials Center was among the first to introduce a series of color cards for the catalog to represent the different formats. Thus, from the start, catalog cards for all of the "audiovisual" materials were interfiled with cards for books and other print materials.

How does a library of some 30,000 items like ours prove that it is a laboratory? John Church has put it well:

> The materials from which the curriculum is planned and developed are the guides to what is in essence education. The Administration that makes these materials for curriculum construction available greatly influences the pattern of education in our culture.[4]

Availability is, of course, the first requirement for a curriculum materials center. But we do not consider availability to mean merely a passive, retrieval function. We believe the center can actively influence pre-service and in-service teacher education in a number of ways.

At the point of materials selection, for example, we have created something called the Faculty Interest Profile. You will recognize this FIP as an old but modernized librarianship technique. Taking a cue from information science as practiced in many industrial technical information centers, we have cataloged faculty research in progress, teaching units, and even personal hobbies. We attempt to match these profiles by continually calling attention to new media related to faculty interests. If we had the staff, we would do what industry does: continuously KWIC index and abstract current related literature that pours into the Materials Center, giving special attention to ephemera not adequately indexed or annotated anywhere. And perhaps, some day, we can utilize the computer center's 1401, as we now do on a limited scale in Library School instruction, to provide printouts to match profiles.

At the point of materials utilization, a more subtle effort goes on hourly with our faculty peers. Unless this peership relation is carefully protected, bibliographic counselling can be jeopardized. It is perfectly human that none of us wants to be exposed as either unaware or outdated. I recall an incident, many years back, when a very good botany teacher was simply unaware of time-lapse photography and what it could do for his teaching. From long association, I knew he was sensitive and that he became defensive when a colleague undertook to educate him about anything in his subject field. I approached him one day like this: "Sam, a new film has been sent us for appraisal. It's in botany, a subject I know very little about. Will you preview this film for me so we can send them an intelligent evaluation?" This immediately recognized him as an authority in his specialty. When he saw the film, through time-lapse, reveal how a flower opens up, he was visibly impressed. From that time on, he became a very heavy user, not only of our film library, but of many other materials.

Ray Lyman Wilbur, the former Stanford president, was once quoted: "Changing the curriculum is like moving a cemetery. No matter how long what's there has been dead, it still has a lot of friends." Curriculum development unquestionably still suffers from the dead hand of the past. But curriculum construction is also restricted by pre-commitments related to habits of thinking. There are those among us who accept without challenge the prescriptive rights of the so-called "tough subjects"—math, science, foreign languages. And there is, of course, much to be said for their recently re-accented curriculum place. But a bit of historical perspective, like materials center counselling, can convince anyone that many of today's favored subjects were less favored yesterday, and may drop to a less respectable position tomorrow.

In the past, the philosophy of curriculum librarianship has been, to too great an extent, to follow the curriculum in selecting materials. This is still a good half of professional principles of materials selection and utilization. But curriculum developers should also remember that what we want to transmit from one generation to the next is the best that man has thought and done; and the record of that "best" is in a good library, such as the curriculum materials center should be. That being so, might not a coordinate principle be that the curriculum should follow the library? An equally basic philosophy of curriculum librarianship should perhaps be to select materials so creatively and to instruct the users so fully, that the curriculum will have to follow the library. Indeed, with the trend to independent study, is it inconceivable that somewhere, someday, a school will declare, "Behold our curriculum, it is our library; behold our library, it is our curriculum." It is conceivable, however, only if a new generation of media teachers comes to our schools.

In 40 years, now, of educational librarianship, the most persistent professional question I have ever heard from my colleagues is: "How can we get teachers to use the library in their teaching?" I agree that this question takes precedence over "How can we get pupils to use the library in their learning?" Probably no pedagogical demagogue will arrive at a convention to proclaim vindictively, "but the children come first." For if we want the children to use the library, the teachers will have to learn to do so first.

We are all aware of the valiant efforts of librarians in the past. To some of us the critical point has been in the selection and acquisition of materials. We have attempted to involve the teacher in the process with innumerable variations on the lures of selection. Faculty committees to represent all grades and subjects have been activated. But commendable as these efforts are, they are all in-service tries.

The next generation of media teachers must be prepared in the curriculum libraries, laboratories, materials centers, or whatever you choose to label them, both on and off campus. The fact remains that materials *per se* do not yet have the status in our teacher education curricula that is accorded to method, subject, curriculum, administration, or learning psychology. Media study in our professional education courses is still largely incidental to all of the other aspects of teacher education.

Until such curriculum recognition is accorded to media in teacher education, the challenge to educate a generation of media teachers must be taken up by our curriculum materials center. We must not only collect, house, organize and circulate materials, but we must interpret these collections in such a way that we equip our colleagues to know these media, *per se*, as well as we do. In this way we will influence their approach to method, subject, learning, curriculum and administration. In short, the dynamic role open to curriculum librarianship transcends any description thus far accorded it. There is the distinct possibility that curriculum librarianship can revolutionize our schools of tomorrow by developing a whole new generation of media teachers.

No one can observe the present trend to independent study without realizing that a new relationship to students faces the next generation of teachers. It is a relationship that is basically bibliographic counselling. To prepare teachers for this new role, I invite curriculum librarians to accept a new challenge. I invite you to prepare a generation of media teachers to guide our next generation of children and young people to independent study in the library.

FOOTNOTES

1. R. E. Browne, "Curriculum Libraries and Laboratories in California," *Bulletin* of the California State Department of Education, Vol. 30, No. 1 (1961), pp. 85-86.

2. Louis Shores, *Instructional Materials* (New York, Ronald Press, 1960).

3. D. S. McVean, "Report of an Evaluation of Curriculum Laboratory Services in a Teacher College," *Journal of Educational Research*, 53:341-44 (1960).

4. J. G. Church, "Creating a Curriculum Laboratory," *California Education*, 1:21 (1964).

AV PATTERNS IN LIBRARY SCHOOL PROGRAMS

ALA-accredited graduate schools of education for librarianship were slow to incorporate audiovisual instruction. In 1954 Florida State was out of line: basic audiovisual courses were required of all candidates for the library master's degree, and AV courses were offered to students majoring in education and other areas in the university. In addition, however, the Library School administers the university's audiovisual services and provides, through the materials center, a demonstration of the unified concept of instructional materials.

There appear to be three patterns to the growing emphasis on audiovisual instruction in library school curricula. For the sake of simplicity, these may be identified as 1) campus-coordinated; 2) library-school-limited; and 3) library-school-extended.

The campus-coordinated program is one in which the library school utilizes the campus facilities, both service and instructional. On some campuses this may mean using the university audiovisual center, which is usually administered by the extension division, the school of education, or the university library. A separate course, usually offered in the school of education, is then adapted through such units as are integrated in the basic library school courses. In this pattern library schools emphasize units as part of selection, organization, and other basic professional library courses. A separate whole course in audiovisual is permitted as an elective and is usually offered outside the library school.

The library-school-limited program appears to be favoring a separate (although perhaps small) audiovisual demonstration unit within the library school. The courses of instruction may include both units in the basic library courses and a separate course or two in audiovisual.

The library-school-extended program undertakes a considerable audiovisual service not only to the library school but perhaps to the campus and even to the state or region which the campus serves. The instructional program will include not only units in the basic library school courses but also several separate courses in the audiovisual fields designed not only for librarians but for teachers, journalists, business people, and any others interested.

The audiovisual program at Florida State University may be considered in the library-school-extended class. It began in 1946, when the Library School set out, with its own opaque projector and limited representative items of equipment and materials in the other audiovisual categories, to demonstrate the basic unit of instructional media of communication to its librarians in training and to teachers in the School of Education. Since several other departments of the campus were then interested in using audiovisual materials (principally 16mm films) in their instruction, and since there was no audiovisual agency on the campus, the Library School was asked to extend its

Reprinted with permission from *AALS Newsletter*, July 1954, pp. 16-19.

audiovisual service to all departments on campus. Upon proper budgetary provisions by the University, the Library School undertook to do this; today the Audio-Visual Center, a so-called Materials Center, and a State Film Rental Library are administered by the Library School.

Briefly, the services directed by the Library School may be divided into two parts: 1) the Audio-Visual Center, which is largely responsible for maintenance, operation, and production; and 2) the Materials Center, which handles dissemination.

The Audio-Visual Center is headed by a director who is also Professor of Audio-Visual in the Library School. He has a staff of ten full-time assistants and several student assistants and service projectionists. The audiovisual service includes: 1) maintenance of all audiovisual equipment, including projectors and all sound equipment; 2) motion picture projection service on the campus; 3) photographic service; 4) public address systems; 5) tape and disc recordings; 6) slide production; 7) some motion picture and filmstrip production (notably filming the football games); 8) film rental library; and 9) microphotographic service. The budget of the Audio-Visual Center is set up separately from the Library School instruction budget, but it is administered by the Dean of the Library School.

The Materials Center is a demonstration of an integrated audiovisual and printed materials library service. It serves both as the Library School Library and as a demonstration Materials Center for the School of Education. Its budget, too, is set up separately but is administered by the Dean of the Library School. The Director of the Materials Center is a professionally trained librarian also qualified in audiovisual. Her staff consists of one full-time assistant, six graduate assistants, and perhaps ten undergraduate student assistants.

The Department of Instruction in Audio-Visual is a department of the Library School. It has three full-time faculty members, and the Head of the Department also serves as Director of the Audio-Visual Center. The faculty in this department plan, with the other faculty members of the Library School, the audiovisual units that are integrated into the basic Library School courses. They also plan the basic audiovisual course required of all librarians—namely, course 426, Audio-Visual Materials. In addition, specialization is offered in the audiovisual field; to date 14 master's degrees with audiovisual majors have been issued. In order that the program of instruction may be seen in relation to the overall Library School program, the outline of the units and separate courses are presented in sequence.

The faculty is continually reviewing the place of audiovisual in the Library School curriculum and is even now engaged in the further refinement of correlating the various units and courses. One of the difficulties encountered in separate courses is planning content so that it will be equally suitable for librarians and school teachers, since the program serves the School of Education as well as the Library School. This is exactly the opposite of the pattern in which the library school goes to the school of education for its audiovisual course. In order to make this effective for both the School of Education and the Library School, a joint faculty committee on instruction and another joint faculty committee on the Materials Center periodically reconsider the school's program. They take into account both professional librarianship requirements and the changing teacher's certification requirements, since the state of Florida is attempting to replace the separate school library and school audiovisual certification with a unified instructional materials certification.

FLORIDA STATE UNIVERSITY LIBRARY SCHOOL

Audio-Visual Content Required of All Library School Graduates

1. Units in L.S. 315, Introduction to Materials
   a. Recordings for children
   b. Flat pictures, slides, filmstrips for storytelling
   c. Selection aids for AV materials

2. Units in L.S. 327, Organization and Administration
   a. Picture file and art collection
   b. Acquisition, cataloging, processing of:
       1) Recordings, simple records, record albums
       2) Films
       3) Filmstrips
       4) Maps
       5) Slides, stereographs, etc.

THE EDUCATION OF THE MEDIA SPECIALIST

Four curriculum areas for the professional preparation of the generalist or the specialist are described: 1) media, as the generic book, approached not only via subject and level, but by format; 2) information, representing a modulation of traditional reference and neo-information science; 3) technique, which comprehends the full range of library, audiovisual, and information science hardware and technical processes; 4) management, with new approaches to administration, organization, personnel, finances, etc.

Call us media specialists, if you will, for want of a better professional label and definition. We are, indeed, specialists in the maintenance and management of media programs. We work in schools and colleges, in communities, states and nations, in industry and in government, and in places and kinds of institutions too numerous even to categorize.

The materials of our work we have recently renamed "media." Webster defines the singular of this word as "a channel of communication." The media specialist deals with all channels of communication. He does not favor print in hard covers, or even paperback, over all other channels. Nor does he work as though the 16mm film, like Duz, does everything that needs to be done educationally. He may have cameras as a personal hobby, or be a ham radio operator on the side, or perform part-time as a disc jockey at a local radio station, or be an oral historian with magnetic tape, or lift opaques from magazine covers to make transparency overlays for the overhead. But if he is a true media specialist, he is not like the six blind men in the fable, each of whom described the whole elephant in terms of the part he happened to touch. No. The media specialist is concerned with all channels of communication. He is involved with what I have called the generic book—all of the media in all of their physical forms. By this definition, a motion picture is as much a part of the generic book as is last week's issue of *Newsweek*. In brief, the generic book is the sum total of man's communication possibilities; it is his evidence of life. And it is with this essential of existence that we media specialists deal.

It should go without saying, therefore, that our chief concern is with people. Our mission is to disseminate man's record of achievement, his best ideas, his noblest dreams. As media specialists we are dedicated to promoting human understanding between man and his environment, between man and man, and between man and God. Before we can provide for the education of the media specialist, it is important that we communicate to each other our understanding of what our profession is.

There are differences, of course, among us. Some of you will recall my struggle in the forties and fifties to bring librarians and audiovisualists together. Some have referred to my book, *Instructional Materials*, and to the Florida unified certification as the shotgun marriage. It wasn't easy.

A paper read to the 23rd annual Audio-Visual Institute at the University of Minnesota, Minneapolis, October 2, 1968, and published in *Minnesota Audio-Visual Education*, November 1968.

Separation still has its marchers. Some picket for separate audiovisual centers in our schools and colleges. Others demonstrate against what they call "non-book" materials.

As in our current political, social, and economic differences, the separate extremists often find themselves demonstrating against the same things. It is questionable who opposes more vehemently the U.S. membership in the United Nations—the Russian Communists or the American reactionaries. Whose opposition to the U.S. involvement in the Vietnam War is more violent—that of the Peking Red Guard or that of the Washington pacifists? Who would be more shocked at the suggestion that North Vietnam, more than South Vietnam, needs a coalition imposed upon it?

So it has frequently been in the differences among media specialists. Extremist librarians and extremist audiovisualists have frequently found themselves supporting each other for separate libraries and separate AV centers. More recently, other separatists have weakened us further: ETV enthusiasts have tended to move away from AV control, or even coordination; information scientists of the separatist camps have been inclined to pick up their computers and walk away from reference librarians. In such divisiveness we all suffer, and the common cause we have to advance—communication among learners and investigators—is unnecessarily handicapped.

So I begin my plea for unity. Whether our major designation in the past has been librarian or audiovisualist, information scientist or televisionist, photographer or archivist, or any of a score or more of specialisms, let us not forget our larger commitment to human understanding through the choice of media. Let us be aware that the format—that is, the physical makeup of the medium—may affect human understanding. This is the only significant point, in my opinion, that Marshall McLuhan makes in all of the furor he has stirred up. Others among us who have understood the deeper potential of our unified profession have stated this again and again, orally at meetings, and in writing for our professional literature. We owe McLuhan gratitude for accomplishing some penetration among those who control the purse strings. But we must differ when he underestimates one of the most significant media formats—print.

In the education of the media specialist, therefore, I believe we must begin by understanding not only media, but people. At the outset, we must overview the channels through which man gives evidence of life by communicating. We must expose the dominant aim of this divine profession of ours: to help people better understand each other and their environment, and even to explore the possibility of the supernatural. To this end, the media specialist serves as a medium between people and media. He does this by understanding individual differences in media sufficiently so that he can match them to the individual differences in people.

He can do this only if he appreciates the whole range of media, impartially, and does not commit himself in advance to one format, or one level, or one subject. And these three—format, level, and subject—suggest the fundamental approach to the study of media that should be undertaken by the specialist, both at the outset and throughout his career. If you say that this approach is more likely to make a generalist of him, rather than a specialist, I agree, and without apology. In this world of increasing specialisms, growing frustrations call out for a *gestalt* that will restore balance and perspective. It is such a courageous and high role I hold out for him who would work with media: the essence of communicability, the evidence of life. A French general commented during World War I that "death is instant incommunicability"; if this is so, then life must be communicability.

Well, shall we then be called media generalists, instead of media specialists? I don't know what to call us. I tried, during the great professional debate between audiovisualists and librarians, to find an occupational label that both groups would accept, since the audiovisualists did not want to be called librarians, and the librarians did not want to be called audiovisualists. Let's settle on media specialist as the name, and continue with the education.

For an appreciation of the whole range of media, I think the specialist should first overview the variety of formats. At one time I counted at least 100 different forms of instructional materials in our nation's schools, ranging from textbook to television, from paperback to projection, from chalkboard to computer console. Because of the number and variety of physical forms among today's media, I undertook my "format classification" for the book *Instructional Materials*.

In this overview, the prospective media specialist should consider print as a channel. He should examine at least five major categories, their strengths and weaknesses in communication, their special contributions in peculiar learning and understanding situations, both within formal education and outside of it. The textbook, for example, despite the debunking efforts of some educators, still has a key position among channels of learning. Serials, including magazines and newspapers, have a distinct communication function. Of all the underestimated media formats among teachers and pupils none has been more tragically neglected than the reference book. There are still some librarians and audiovisualists, for example, who are unaware of the new dimensions introduced into transparency overlays by some of the major encyclopedias. Nor must the potential of the reading book be ignored, despite our current interest in "where the action is."

Although the major category of graphics has been generously represented in both library science and audiovisual instruction, not all of its components have been equally exploited. Both librarians and audiovisualists claim maps and globes, but neither group of special specialists has made much of these "place media" *par excellence.* Perhaps because I have circled the globe several times, by air, sea, and land—but probably because I really believe maps are better than marches as media for peace—I feel we media specialists have done an inadequate job with these formats. It may be no index at all, but at one of these increasingly and encouragingly frequent joint meetings of librarians and audiovisualists, a Rand McNally speaker was unable to get an answer to his question, "What is an analemma?" Perhaps we have learned to communicate time and season and region effectively without this term?

When it comes to projections, all of us tend to "procrusteate" our communicands to our favorite format. I confess to a weakness for the transparency overlay. All of my colleagues can tell when I am starting off for my extension class downstate, because I tuck an overhead under my arm as I go out the door. You know the slide addicts, caricatured by the suffering next-door neighbors who resignedly sigh, "Here come some more lost weekends. The Joneses have just returned from their vacation, and we'll be seeing slides till they run out of our eyes."

Just as some librarians resist the 16mm format, many audiovisualists are reluctant to use microforms. Of course, a microfilm is a projection, and what the librarian calls a reader is a projector. Furthermore, there are at least three other micro-projections of print and graphics; two of these are opaque, and the third is transparent. Why the audiovisualist hasn't claimed all four, instead of permitting the librarian to become possessive about them, is another of the ambiguities in the effort to separate audiovisual and library materials. Before a sensitive audiovisualist reminds me, let me hasten to add that there are, of course, additional kinds of micro-projections.

And when it comes to the major category I call transmissions, the sensitive librarian will be quick to remind me that libraries had phonograph records in their collections long before there was even an audiovisual movement—or an audiovisualist to rename these formats "discs." Nor has the magnetic tape been outside the librarian's domain. Librarians have been in the vanguard of the oral history movement, which gave the hardware one of its first softwares.

To the media specialist, there is no reason for either sensitivity—that of the audiovisualist or that of the librarian. We are all in this together. We have in our profession the greatest potential for the prevention of human catastrophe. We can, if we know the whole range of our media, do a most effective job of advancing human understanding by matching individual and group differences in people with individual and group differences in media. But we can't do that if we insist on segregation among us, or if we relegate the media we don't favor to the back seats in the omnibus. Some audiovisualists do this with print; some librarians do this with "non-print." Any of us with liberal spirit have come to distrust the statement that "some of my best friends are . . . ." The librarian's counterpart to this thought is, "I go to movies often, but students have got to study books." Or the observation by some audiovisualists, "Teachers already know books; what they need to know is AV." The media specialist says that what both teachers and pupils need to know are media of all shapes, sizes, colors, etc. The simple fact that people watch TV every night does not guarantee that they know the format well enough to gain understanding from it. The fact that many read the newspaper daily, or a book infrequently, is no assurance that they know how to gather understanding from these media formats.

Without enumerating any of the other media formats, and with the hope that the citing of just a few will not be taken as an indication of favoring them, let me emphasize that the education of the media specialist must introduce him at the very outset to all of the formats, before he can become attached to any one.

The same must be done for the other two approaches to understanding media. Through a library classification like Dewey or Library of Congress, the student of media can get an overview of all subjects, in the proper perspective, that the subject specialist rarely has. In this way, he will avoid the academic snobbery that so often occurs on our campuses: "My subject is substantive; yours is ancillary." Right now the sciences are riding the crest. Time was when they ranked far below Latin, theology, or philosophy. Right now the social sciences are pushing for respectability by adopting the sacred methods of natural science, although education is still considered as a stepchild. Parapsychology, already excommunicated by psychology, has been put on probation by the physical and biological sciences. (I have no doubt, however, that the great and good Dr. Rhine will console himself.)

Finally, in this first overview course, the media specialist must be introduced to media levels. The extensive range of maturity among the people who communicate accounts for many individual differences, so media level is as important as the format or the subject. Neither the chronologic nor the mental age can any longer be considered all-important. There are other factors. Consider the public library evidence that, when it comes to science subjects, many eight- and nine-year-old boys have to go to the adult department for books that will be at all informative and challenging, while most adults, to keep from bewilderment, sheepishly come to the children's department for their science information.

Consider some of the finger-whistlers in the audience of popular television programs. I prefer to believe that our national mind is not quite that low, and that the networks, in response to the appeal to employ the physically handicapped, preferred instead to provide entertainment for the mentally handicapped. Certainly, a disproportionate number of commercials reflect the low estimate of American mentality that advertising agencies have. If they are right, then our job as media specialists is really critical. If the people of the United States can really be sold on commercial products by the sub-mental appeals that interrupt unaesthetic programs, then the communists are really asleep at the subversion switch. All they need is a corny jingle or two and they can take over without firing a shot.

Here is a real challenge to us as media specialists. If we know our levels in media as well as in people, we can start at the finger-whistler's present level and, by the device librarians call the "ladder list," can lead him skillfully but painlessly, step by step, to better things. At the very least, we can provide him with some comparisons for a deliberate choice. I submit that one of the keenest challenges before us as media specialists is to help toughen our American national mind. From the beginning of the education of the media specialist, I want us to become aware of the range of our working materials, of the formats, subjects, and levels of our media so that we may, like the good physician, match individual differences for communication in people.

If the first major area of our professional curriculum is media, then perhaps the second might be designated "information." Librarians of the traditional school have called this "reference," and I have redefined this term as meaning "the promotion of free inquiry." In the past, librarians have undertaken to answer questions through basic reference books. Now, the reference book is a unique medium. It is different from most books, because it is not meant to be read from cover to cover. These media formats are still the best tools for fact-finding, for documenting issues, and even for working crossword puzzles, answering questions on quiz programs, or preparing for national examinations. If it is true that the librarian has neglected the motion picture as a medium, it is equally true that the audiovisualist has certainly not learned much about the reference book.

In recent years, a counterpart to the audiovisual-librarianship schism has appeared in the form of information science. Breaking somewhat with the tradition of the reference librarian, the information scientist, like his revolutionary predecessor, the audiovisualist, introduced some new dimensions. To the conservative librarian, both the audiovisualist and the information scientist are primarily concerned with hardware. Just as the projector was for the librarian the trademark of the audiovisualist, the computer is the symbol of the information scientist.

Fortunately, there are many librarians who have appreciated what both the audiovisual and the information science revolutions have meant to the broader professional aim of the media specialist. Not since the introduction of the Gutenberg printing press in the fifteenth century has any phenomenon had a more profound impact on communication than the inauguration of the audiovisual concept, toward the end of the nineteenth century. Traditional librarians resisted both innovations. Edgar Dale has quoted the fifteenth century librarian who declared that his was a real library, because it had only handwritten manuscripts—none of these newfangled machine-produced things called "print." Four centuries later, some librarians paraphrase these words when they declare that "this is a real library; no 'non-book' materials are here." Some of my fellow librarians, and all of my students, know how allergic I am to the term "non-book."

Right after World War II, another communication revolution came along. Like audiovisualism before it, information science has too often neglected to look at traditional library science. As a result, the information scientist, like the audiovisualist, has frequently underestimated the librarian. Just as some audiovisualists refer to "flat pictures" as if libraries never devoted themselves to picture collection and dissemination; or to "discs," without realizing that the Carnegie Corporation endowed phono-record service in libraries, so the information scientist today goes about with his new vocabulary unaware that the genesis of the idea can be found in traditional reference. For example, the tremendously fine concept of SDI (Selective Dissemination of Information) was practiced by the traditional reference librarian, albeit somewhat crudely and under a different name. The origins of what the information scientist calls KWIC indexing (Key Word in Context) can be discovered in what the German librarians called *Schlagwort*. But the fact remains that the information scientist, like the audiovisualist before him, has added a new dimension to communication. He has done this not alone through the drama of the digital computer, but through his creative concepts of system design, of interest profiles, of research in the information-gathering habits of scientists.

But the information scientist's hazard is the separatist complex that has handicapped so many audiovisualists and librarians before him. Like his predecessors in the separatist camps, the information scientist has not yet identified himself in the broader profession of communication. He does not yet consider himself a media specialist.

Seeking to avoid some of the pains in that long struggle to unite audiovisualists with librarians in our common cause, I sought, for our faculty, an information scientist who had also been trained in traditional library science. I found a research chemist who had gone on to take the basic library science master's, then a Ph.D. that included advanced library science. In the past five years, he has accomplished what I call a sensitive modulation from traditional reference librarianship to modern information science. Dr. Gerald Jahoda has already produced some media specialists with excellent mastery of our information techniques. It didn't take long for his student majors to begin calling themselves "Jahoda's Witnesses."

As a third area in the curriculum for media specialists, I suggest "technique" as a simple overall title. Librarians call their comparable area "technical processes." In it they include acquisitions, classification, and cataloging, as well as technology especially related to library automation, to equipment, to hardware, and to facilities. This area, broadened, would comprehend all the knowledge and skills of equipment maintenance, operation, procurement, and media production.

The fourth major area in the curriculum for media specialists would concern management. All of the problems of organizing and administering media programs in all kinds of institutions would be studied here. Special attention would be given to libraries of every type; to audiovisual centers, when they are separate; and to technical information centers when information scientists operate them separately. Service to every type of community would be considered—to cities, states, regions, and nations; to schools and colleges; to industry and government. Studies of users, by age, occupation, location, sex, cultures, etc., would receive discriminating review. The media specialist himself would be evaluated—his emerging status, professional associations, publications, ethics, rewards, and all his segmented groups.

Fitting the education of the media specialist into practice and education, I see four levels of preparation above the clerical. That there is a need for a clerical level is more than ordinarily apparent. Too many professionals among media specialists, in all segments, are engaged in activities that are hardly professional. Typing catalog cards, splicing films, or key punching tapes, should hardly require hours a day of the time of master's degree librarians, audiovisualists, and information scientists. A high school graduate with commercial training can adequately perform most of these duties and tasks.

There is, however, a paraprofessional level of duties requiring more education than the clerical, but less than the professional. For librarians, these tasks have been specified by the U.S. Civil Service Commission's GS-1411 series. Comparable levels of work can be found both in audiovisual centers and in technical information centers. Education for the paraprofessional media aide should be based on junior college graduation that includes semi-professional education in the media area.

When it comes to professional media preparation, I see three levels. At the first professional level, I place the teacher, or librarian, or audiovisualist, or information scientist. His basic professional preparation should be encompassed within the four-year college bachelor's degree. It can be based on the Junior College Aide program, or it can begin with the junior year. Within the 125 semester hours of course work that is standard for the bachelor's degree, about 30 should be allocated to beginning courses in the four curriculum areas suggested. This should be done without apology to the purists in liberal arts. Nowhere in Genesis is there any documentation that proves some predatory subjects are more substantive, or more "liberal," than others. But this is the subject of another whole essay on the meaning of education in general.

At the second and higher professional levels, the specialist practitioner will have post-bachelor education to match his responsibilities. A master's degree will be minimum; a sixth-year post-master's desirable; a doctorate reinforcing. His preparation will include advanced work in the four areas, plus increasing specialization in a media format (such as telelvision, computer-assisted instruction, reference books), in an aspect of information (such as systems design), in techniques (such as media production), or in a phase of management (such as personnel).

The specialist instructor or researcher will accent research in his post-bachelor work, rather than practice. His professional objective will be to advance the frontiers of knowledge in communication. He may choose psychology as his major collateral, and increasingly, if he is a courageous visionary, parapsychology. Because the future may yet discover that learning is more extrasensory than sensory.

In outline here is an education for the media specialist that will draw us together in our common cause. The detail can develop through great professional conversation. Once librarians, audiovisualists, and information scientists begin to prepare together for their common profession, we will be on our way to something greater than anything we now have. Once each of our segments begins to appreciate the other two, there will be less condescension. Until that time, we will continue to educate librarians, audiovisualists, and information scientists, rather than media specialists.

Because I believe the media specialist comprehends the other three, and because I do not think we can attain our lofty objective without an impartial knowledge of all the media formats, I strongly advocate a unified education for all media specialists. With this broader preparation, we can go on to advance human understanding and tolerance, and thus do our share to hasten the coming of the Kingdom.

APPENDIX

APPENDIX

SOME LANDMARKS ALONG THE WAY

TO MEDIA UNITY, 1936-1969

1936–1940

Peabody Library School introduced the first audiovisual course for librarians. Dr. Milton Lanning Shane, Professor of Modern Languages, attracted by the potential of records, filmstrips, and films for teaching modern languages, shared his enthusiasm with the director of the Library School, who was similarly and concurrently aroused by the possibilities of these new formats for librarianship. Together they planned the course that was to be offered in the Library School—primarily for modern language teachers and librarians, but also for other teaching majors.

1946–1949

Florida State University activated the "School of Library Training and Service," subsequently renamed the Library School, and then the School of Library Science. It was one of the first three graduate schools for the education of librarians that was accredited under the new ALA Standards (the other two were Indiana and Texas).

Integral to the Florida State program was the introduction of the idea that all librarians should be educated audiovisually. Not readily accepted in the post-World War II years was the philosophical concept of the "generic book," which did not limit the definition of a book to print, but contended that just as clay tablets, parchment, and other formats had preceded the Gutenberg book, so also newer book formats (like photograph, slide, filmstrip, disc, tape, radio, TV, community resource, teaching machine, and computer-assisted instructional devices) had followed it.

In order that librarians might be prepared to disseminate books not only in all subjects and for all levels of maturity, but also in the entire range of formats, Florida State University introduced into its curriculum a required course in media or, as these were then referred to, "instructional materials."

One of the earliest publications to support this course was developed by several Florida State University Library School faculty members under the authorship of the noted audiovisual authority, C. F. Hoban. He had been appointed full-time professor in 1947—probably the first such appointment to a library school faculty. According to one reviewer, the book, *The Audiovisual Way* (Tallahassee, Florida State Department of Education, Bulletin No. 22B, January 1948. 118p.) was the best book on audiovisual education, despite the fact that it had been created in a school of library science. Dr. Hoban, together with his father and Dr. S. B. Zisman, was also the author of the standard audiovisual textbook used in teacher education institutions.

1950-1959

Spearheaded by the FSU Library School and the Florida State Department of Education, giant steps were taken toward unifying librarians and audiovisualists in their common cause.

The Library School joined the School of Education in developing a series of summer "Leadership Institutes" for school personnel—supervisors, principals, teachers, librarians, and audiovisualists. Out of these institutes emerged two Florida Education Association sections—FAVA (Florida Audio-visual Association) and FASL (Florida Association of School Librarians)—that were increasingly committed to unity. They began meeting for a joint luncheon at the annual FEA convention in the spring. The FSU Library School hosted a joint fall meeting (for ten years) in the Library School, where differences and agreements were considered.

In cooperation with the State Department of Education, the first unified certification was developed—"No. 18" in the series of state certification requirements as published in the State Department of Education certification handbook. "No. 18" (as revised and adopted on March 20, 1962) is reprinted below.

18.   Library and Audio-Visual Service (Instructional Materials)—Grades 1–12.

Certification is granted in the field of Library and Audio-Visual Service on two plans, either of which will certify an applicant for work with printed and audio-visual materials. The training in this section may be provided in separate courses or in comprehensive courses as the training institutions may determine with the approval of the Florida State Department of Education. Relationship of all types of instructional materials should be emphasized in any type of course organization.

Plan 1. Library and Audio-Visual Service (Grades 1–12) will be placed on the face of a certificate when a total of 30 semester hours in Library Service and related courses has been earned. These 30 semester hours must include:

1) Books and Related Materials for Young People 6
2) Organization and Administration of
    School Libraries or Materials Centers 6
3) Reference Materials 2
4) Classification and Cataloging 2
5) Audio-Visual Materials 2

The remainder of the 30 semester hours may be taken in other library courses or courses in the following areas: remedial reading, reading guidance, story telling, and audio-visual education.

Plan 2. Applicants who qualify for the Provisional Graduate or higher type certificate covering Elementary Education and/or one or more secondary school teaching fields will qualify for certification in Instructional Materials (Library and Audio-Visual Service) with 21 semester hours of credit as follows:

1) Books and Related Materials for Young People 6
2) Organization and Administration of
     School Libraries or Materials Centers 6
3) Reference Materials 2
4) Classification and Cataloging 2
5) Audio-Visual Materials 3
6) Preparation, Production, and Use of
     Instructional Materials 2

Among the requirements was a common, basic course in Instructional Materials to be required not only of librarians and audiovisualists, but of elementary teachers as well. In the early days this was known as the famous "315," an augmented children's literature course that moved steadily toward introducing librarians and teachers to the whole range of book formats—print, graphic, projection, transmission, resource, etc. This course was pioneered by two members of the Library School faculty—Professors Agnes Gregory and Sara (Krentzman) Srygley—who led in the effort to balance the content. Among the faculty audiovisualists who contributed were Dr. Hoban, Amo DeBernardis, Myles Ritchie, Otis McBride, William J. Quinly, Harold Moreland, and others. In addition to Professor Gregory and Professor Srygley, some outstanding school librarians who served as regular or visiting faculty helped in the integration of print and audiovisual materials and perspective: Louise Galloway, Ruth Rockwood, Elenora Alexander, and others.

Course organization at times became a tug of war. Partisan librarians tended to continue their accustomed "children's literature" accent with a few "non-books" appended. Equally biased audiovisualists wanted films, transparency overlays, discs, radio, TV, graphics, *et al.*, for nearly 100 percent of the content, since, as one put it, "they already know how to read books." Despite near-feuds at times, the course developed toward true integration of formats.

To practice the media unity that the Library School was teaching, it was decided to activate a new kind of library school library, to be called a "materials center." This same term was used as the title of State Department of Education Bulletin 22C, by Professor Srygley, who had been one of the first to understand and communicate the concept of the materials center. Assisting her was a group of pioneer librarians, audiovisualists, classroom teachers, and educational administrators who had been converted to the mission of media unity. These pioneers contributed greatly to the cause of media unity that was so strongly resisted by some separatists in the post-World War II years.

Inevitably, to impress on librarians, audiovisualists, and teachers that all of these formats were books—variations in the physical makeup of the generic book–a unified catalog was needed. Mrs. Bess Daughtry, librarian of the Materials Center, developed such a catalog and published *Classifying and Cataloging Audiovisual Materials* (Tallahassee, Florida State University, 1950). Colors (blue for films, yellow for slides, pink for discs, etc.) were introduced into the card catalog for the first time, in order to distinguish the different formats in the card catalog. An early effort was made to standardize entry form in each case; others later refined these beginnings.

One major concern was housing and equipping this emerging variation on the idea of a library. The first Materials Center home was an old barracks building; next, a campus residence was taken over; and finally, part of the basement of the new Strozier Library was converted to demonstrate some of the ultimate features. What could not be accomplished was written into some specifications for a new State Department of Education bulletin.

Louise Galloway, chairman of the committee for planning this bulletin, had come to the Florida State University Library School from the Kentucky Department of Education, where she had served as school library supervisor. She had, indeed, contributed to publications on housing both in Kentucky and in the Philippines, where she had been consultant. Because she understood and practiced the unity concept, she was an ideal person both for teaching Library School extension classes that carried the gospel to all corners of the state, and for chairing the production of the housing bulletin.

In this bulletin were some of the germs of the later ideas for planning learning resource centers. How to relate print to film, disc, graphics, etc., is indicated in the principles of planning and equipping a materials center. In embryo, also, are the beginning designs for independent study in carrels, with a range of media formats.

The Florida Instructional Materials Clinics, under the joint sponsorships of the Florida State University Library School, the Florida State Department of Education, and the General Extension Division of Florida, were staged in seven strategic locations from Pensacola in the northwest to Key West in the southeast. During each of the pre-school conferences (1955, 1956, and 1957), over 1,500 Florida teachers, administrators, librarians, audiovisualists, and instructional materials specialists participated.

At each location the one-day conference consisted of what I called a "Medium Fair"–a gigantic exhibit of current and retrospective media of all formats, subjects, and levels from K through 14 (to cover the needs of Florida's emerging community junior colleges).

Formats on display ranged from textbooks through television. From the "print kingdom" there were encyclopedias and yearbooks, dictionaries, atlases, and other reference books. The serial division displayed recommended periodicals and newspapers, government publications, and pamphlet series and separates.

Graphics displayed featured charts and graphs, pictures (from art reproductions to comics and cartoons), and photography. Dioramas, coming into vogue, murals, and illustrations of all kinds were supported by "museum objects," more excitingly called "realia" by some audiovisualists. These objects were samplings from most of the categories. Exhibit and display were prominent everywhere, especially emphasizing the various boards–chalk, peg, flannel, and magnetic.

Projections subtly reminded librarians that microtexts—film, card, fiche, print—illustrated what the audiovisualist classified as "opaque" and "transparent," and belonged with filmstrip and motion picture as well as with transparency overlays and, of course, slides, which libraries had accessioned long ago. Even the 1950s rage for three-dimensional pictures had been anticipated by what libraries had projected in the old-fashioned stereopticon.

Transmissions were richly represented by phonograph "discs" (as the audiovisualists had begun to call them to distinguish them from the librarians' "records"). There were tapes and transcriptions of radio programs, kinescopes of television classics, and live radio and television.

Programmed media were in their beginnings, consisting chiefly of teaching machines both in hardware and in print, and some halting first steps with computer-assisted instruction. Florida State Library School had just begun its "information science" modulation through my beginning reference course, determined to bridge this new developing schism between traditional librarianship and the newly developing periphery.

Production of materials was a continuous feature of the "medium fair." Experts on our travelling team demonstrated and taught librarians, audiovisualists, and teachers to dry mount, make slides, "lift" a magazine picture to an acetate transparency, photograph for all kinds of learning missions.

The clinics were exciting adventures. They were given added impetus by a tremendous achievement—the result of Florida's success in uniting audiovisualists and librarians in their common cause—the Florida legislature appropriated a million dollars as a supplement earmarked for "instructional materials."

1960–1969

Although die-hard separatists persisted in both the librarian and the audiovisualist camps, unity gained steadily. After the many forums and debates of the late 1950s, illustrated in this book by the reprintings from *Educational Screen* and *NEA Journal*, notable movements to integrate were evident in about a dozen or more state certifications and in the joint efforts of audiovisual and library organizations.

One of the most notable national efforts by an educational organization was undertaken by the National Education Association's ASCD (Association for Supervision and Curriculum Division) about 1960, when it activated a National Commission on Instructional Materials. Membership was recruited from librarianship, audiovisual instruction, educational administration and supervision, publishing, film production, and other media production. Some distinguished leaders from all of these areas contributed to the meetings, including many in the vanguard of media thinking, like Edgar Dale, Paul Witt, and Marshall McLuhan.

Most effective were the joint efforts of school librarians, through their AASL, and the audiovisualists, through their division of the NEA, then known as DAVI (Department of Audiovisual Instruction). Ultimately, in 1969 their combined efforts led to the 1969 Media Standards, a confirmation of the unity program first pioneered in Florida right after World War II.

To further the theory of the generic book on which unity practice was based, numerous oral and written advocacies appeared all over the United States. C. Walter Stone, first at the University of Illinois and later as coordinator of media grants for the U.S. Office of Education, encouraged investigations in the library-media field. McGraw-Hill published an attempt to create a non-print counterpart of the *Cumulative Book Index*, prepared by a committee of librarians and audiovisualists. As so often happens in such colossal undertakings, critics concentrated on minutiae rather than the overall potential for such an undertaking.

Something this media indexing effort pointed out was the need for some cataloging rules for entering audiovisual titles in catalogs and bibliographies. A joint committee, under the chairmanship of William Quinly, member of that Florida State Library School committee that pioneered in the unity concept, issued two preliminary versions of a media cataloging code. Certainly, the work of this committee will refine such cataloging efforts as those of the Library of Congress, the Wilson indexing services, especially the film and filmstrip indexes that preceded the McGraw-Hill imprint, and the entry forms used by the Educators Progress Service of Randolph, Wisconsin.

Media philosophy, theory, and education were advanced during the 1960s by Edgar Dale, Charles Schuller, Paul Witt, Marshall McLuhan, Louis Shores, and others. Dale had brought to the audiovisual field a brilliant background in reading investigation. His "cone of experience" theory laid a foundation for much of the subsequent learning accent on multi-sensory media. Schuller anticipated the impacts of physical format variations on teacher-pupil relations, and McLuhan dramatized the importance of media format in communication. These were important impacts for this author in his developing theory about the "generic book."

In 1960, Ronald Press published *Instructional Materials*, which put together the theory of the generic book and its applications for librarianship, audiovisualism, education, and communication.

1969 AND AFTER

Beginning in 1969, some final confirmations to the concept of media unity were produced jointly by audiovisualists and librarians. In that year appeared the *Standards for School Media Programs*, prepared by the American Association of School Librarians and the Department of Audiovisual Instruction of the National Education Association, in cooperation with representatives from 28 other concerned associations (Chicago, ALA, and Washington, NEA, 1969. 66p.). Florida librarians and audiovisualists glowed with pride over many of the compromises and conciliations.

After the DAVI became the Association for Educational Communications and Technology, the unity mission with librarians, if anything, accelerated creatively. One publication that illustrates the trend to union is *Developing Multi-Media Libraries*, by Warren B. Hicks and Alma M. Tillin. The bibliographic efforts pioneered by Bess Daughtry's 1950 pamphlet, *Cataloging and Classifying Audiovisual Materials* and continued by such agencies as the Library of Congress and the H. W. Wilson Company have been carried forward by the work of a joint committee on cataloging, chaired by William J. Quinly, *Standards for Cataloging Nonprint Materials*, 3rd ed. (Washington, Association for Educational Communications and Technology, 1972. 61p.). The committee has developed an entry form for a wide range of formats—at least 23 major components of the generic book. Section I formulates cataloging rules, and Section II applies them to motion pictures, phonodiscs, charts, microforms, globes, video tapes, records, *et al.* Incidentally, the chairman of the committee has been a Florida State University faculty member since the early days of the unity crusade, and was one of the first audiovisualists with an ALA-accredited librarianship degree.

It has been a long and arduous effort, since 1935, to unite these two highly creative educational groups in our common cause of educating more effectively through media. At times it has appeared that our struggle was lost and the effort was very much in vain. And then along comes a recognition like that on page 265 of Dr. Jesse Shera's monumental book, *Foundations of Education for Librarianship* (Becker and Hayes, 1972): "It was at Peabody, too, that Louis Shores began the development of a program of library school instruction in the audio-visual field that, a few years later, was to achieve fuller development at Florida State University." Perhaps not all of the professional heartache was in vain.

BIBLIOGRAPHY

BiBLIOGRAPHY

The first section of this bibliography consists of "impact readings" for media unity that were published from 1940 to 1969. The second part lists "crusade writings" by the author during that same period. Comprehensive bibliographies on audiovisual librarianship can be found in the reading lists of several library and audiovisual textbooks, and in *Library Literature, Education Index* for those years.

I. IMPACT READINGS

Theory

Brown, J. W., R. B. Lewis, and F. F. Harcleroad. *A V Instruction: Media and Methods*. New York, McGraw-Hill, 1969.

Dale, Edgar. *Audiovisual Methods in Teaching*. New York, Dryden Press, 1946.

Dale, Edgar. "The Challenge of Audiovisual Media." In Louis Shores, *Challenges to Librarianship*. Tallahassee, Florida State University, 1953. pp. 93-106.

Hoban, C.F. *The Audiovisual Way*. Tallahassee, Florida State Department of Education Bulletin 22B, 1948. 118p.

Hoban, C. F., C. F. Hoban, Jr., and S. B. Zisman. *Visualizing the Curriculum*. New York, Dryden Press, 1937.

McLuhan, Marshall. *Understanding Media*. New York, American Library, 1965.

Wittich, Walter, and Charles Schuller. *Audiovisual Materials: Their Nature and Use*. New York, Harper and Row, 1957.

Media Center

Beynon, John. *Study Carrels: Designs for Independent Study Space*. Stanford, Calif., Educational Facilities Laboratories, 1964.

DAVI–AASL. Joint Committee. *Media Standards*. 1968.

DeBernardis, Amo, *et al. Planning Schools for New Media*. Washington, U.S. Office of Education, 1961.

Galloway, Louise. *Planning Materials Centers*. Tallahassee, Florida State Department of Education Bulletin 22E, 1958. 47p.

National Education Association. Department of Audiovisual Instruction. *Planning Schools for Use of Audiovisual Materials*.

Oklahoma Christian College. *The Sound of Learning*. Oklahoma City, 1966. Binder and tape.

Rufsvold, Margaret. *Audiovisual School Library Service*. Chicago, ALA, 1949.

Srygley, Sara K. *The Materials Center*. Tallahassee, Florida State Department of Education Bulletin 22C, 1955. 136p.

Media Selection

Textbooks

American Textbook Publishers Institute. *Textbooks Are Indispensable*. New York, American Textbook Publishers Institute, 1950.

American Textbook Publishers Institute. *Textbooks in Education*. New York, American Textbook Publishers Institute, 1949.

Watt, Lois B. *Textbook Classification Scheme*. Washington, U.S. Office of Education, 1967. 19p.

Reference Books

Handbook for Instructional Leaders on the Use of Encyclopedias in Schools. Seattle, University of Washington, 1956.

Maps and Globes

Harris, Ruby M. *Rand McNally Handbook of Map and Globe Usage*. New York, Rand McNally, 1959.

Community Resources

Bathurst, Effie G. *How Children Use the Community for Learning*. Washington, U.S. Office of Education, 1955.

Fifty Teachers to a Classroom. New York, Macmillan, 1950.

Pictures

Miller, Bruce, and M. B. Osborn. *So You Want to Start a Picture File*. Riverside, Calif., Author, 1964.

Projections

Cypher, Irene. "Filmstrips to Use in the Classroom." Supplement to *Instructor*, 1954.

Taylor, J. Y. *Opaque Projection: A New Frontier in Teaching*. Buffalo, American Optical Company, 1941.

II. CRUSADE WRITINGS

by Louis Shores

"AV Clearing House," *College and Research Libraries* July 1955–July 1956 (monthly department).

"AV Dimensions for an Academic Library," *College and Research Libraries* 1954, pp. 393-97.

"AV Patterns in Library School Programs," *AALS Newsletter*, July 1954, pp. 16-19.

"Books–Continuous Communicability," *Saturday Review*, March 22, 1958, p. 26.

"Enter the Materials Center," *ALA Bulletin*, 1955, pp. 285-88.

"How to Tailor Learning . . . ," *Journal of the Florida Education Association*, Nov. 1954, pp. 12-13ff.

Instructional Materials: An Introduction for Teachers. New York, Ronald Press, 1960. 408p.

"Library and AV Center: Combined or Separate?," *NEA Journal*, May 1958, pp. 342-43.

"Portrait of a Materials Center," *Peabody Journal of Education*, Sept. 1955, pp. 66-74.

"School Library 21," *School Libraries*, May 1963, pp. 11-17.

"Union Now: AV Way and the Library Way," *Educational Screen*, Feb. 9, 1952, pp. 36-39.

"Unity of Materials," a message on tape for the University of Southern California Audiovisual Workshop, 1953.

INDEX

INDEX